Dirty Gold

....

Celine Kopf

Copyright © 2024 by Celine Kopf

All rights reserved.

No portion of this book may be reproduced in any form without written permission from the publisher or author, except as permitted by U.S. copyright law.

Contents

Chapter 1 - The Silver Phoenix	1
Chapter 2 - So It Begins.......	11
Chapter 3 - Cocktails and Four Wheelers	22
Chapter 4 - Juggling Memories	32
Chapter 5 - A Proper Vagabond	40
Chapter 6 - A New World	52
Chapter 7 - Always Respect The Artist	62
Chapter 8 - Friends And Foes Of The Heart	76
Chapter 9 - Teach Me	85
Chapter 10 - Family Ties	98
Chapter 11 - If The Shoe Fits......	108
Chapter 12 - Lies That Bind Part 1	116
Chapter 13 - Lies That Bind Part 2	125
Chapter 14 - Hearts On Fire	138
Chapter 15 - Old Flames & New Habits	151

Chapter 16 - Honest Intentions	162
Chapter 17 - Posh & Becks Part 1	174
Chapter 18 - Posh & Beck Part 2	185
Chapter 19 - Knock You Down	196
Dreaded Authors Note	204
Chapter 20 - Wet Realities	205
Chapter 21 - Ad Infinitum	213
Chapter 22 - Real And True	219
Not An Update But Important	230
Chapter 23 - Green Eyed Dilemma	231
Chapter 24 - Falsetto	241
Chapter 25 - Dear One	250
Chapter 26 - Against The World	257
Chapter 27 - Beautiful Scars On Critical Veins (i)	263
Chapter 28 - Beautiful Scars On Critical Veins (ii)	269
Chapter 29 - Take A Breath, Say You Love Me	279
Chapter 30 - Exhale	286

Chapter 1- The Silver Phoenix

Chapter 1- The Silver Phoenix

"No." I deadpanned to my roommate Pierce as he taunted me for the third time.

"Come on mate it'll be fun, I promise." He begged.

I rose up my hand to stop him "You promising only tells me that this is going to turn out much worse."

Pierce rolled his eyes "Don't be dramatic Kenny. It doesn't always happen like that." I scoffed watching him run his fingers through his blonde quiff. When we first met I teased him endlessly about how much he resembled the Irish dude from that boy band and made sure to sing a demented version of their songs everyday just to piss him off. Which it's such an irony because he's also Irish.

It may also be because I found a poster of the same boy band buried under his bed, which he denies ownership to but I know better.

"You realize that what you're asking me to join you to do is illegal right?" I asked matter-of-factly placing my highlighter behind my ear.

"It's almost midnight no one's gonna know." Pierce tried to negotiate with me.

"Right, the precious time I could be using to sleep or study is when you want to initiate me into a life of crime." I said further to get my point across.

"It's not a crime. We're just going to get on one of those fancy yachts for an hour or so then hop off with no one getting hurt at all." He ended like it was the most logical thing on earth.

"The answer is still no. Plus it is a crime considering the fact that it's private property and we'll be trespassing on it which calls for several points of arrest. And if the owners' nice enough we might not have any charges pressed." I stated clearly for him.

Pierce huffed in what seemed to be annoyance "Sometimes I wonder why you're an English major instead of going for Law. You seem very good at it."

I shrugged trying not to smile smugly at the comment "Eh I guess."

I turned to my textbook in satisfaction thinking that was the end of it but Pierce had other ideas seeing as he plopped himself on my bed without warning.

"Get your ass outta my bed douchebag!" I shouted trying to push him off and save my poor textbook.

He grinned like a Tasmanian devil "Not until you say yes Kenny."

"For the last time I'm not going to help you trash a random boat with your friends!" I yelled right in his face but Pierce didn't even flinch a bit.

He raised an eyebrow "Well I didn't want to do this, but you leave me no choice."

"What are you talking about?" I asked pausing from punching his back to face him in suspicion.

"Good thing I had Mexican for lunch." He said nonchalantly. My look of confusion turned into a look of horror as soon as I understood what he was implying.

"You wouldn't dare." I said lowly narrowing my eyes.

Pierce shrugged then sent me a smug look "Try me." He wiggled his butt which any day I might have pretended not to admire but not it only resembled a plump cannon of destruction.

"I'm warning you-oh shit!" my hands flew to protect my nose as Pierce shamelessly, farted all over my bed and textbook. "Dude you're sick!"

He remained impassive until he was completely done. I glared at him "What the hell is wrong with you?"

"It's the only way I can you to say yes." He replied again smiling as if he hadn't just burnt a smelly hole through my bed. I rolled my eyes "What makes you think I'm going to say yes?"

He shrugged a shoulder "Because you have a nice full closet of thing I could fart on."

My eyes widened "Ok! You win! I'll follow you to the stupid marina if it means you won't spread your dangerous gases all over my room."

Pierce grinned so widely it was a surprise his lips didn't touch his ears "I knew you'd come around Kenny boy."

"Yeah whatever just get out. And stop calling me Kenny dude." I shuffled backwards to lean on my headboard while he stood up.

"It'll be swell I promise!" he called out in his accent. I rolled my eyes mumbling "As long as you don't ever use the word swell again." I was pretty that word was banned since the twenties.

I sighed lying back on one of my pillows. Pierce was a pretty good guy despite his weird tendencies which were to be expected anyway. His parents named him Pierce for goodness sake. I could actually say that he was one of the people who helped me when I first moved here to go to uni. It was challenging leaving my home in Sacramento to come live in London but it was sort of necessary. The scholarship I got also didn't hurt.

I was born and lived my whole life in California which made me eager to explore somewhere far from my comfort zone. Of course I missed my mother terribly but it was something I needed to do on my own.

Now a year later and nothing's made me regret my decision. Well, other than Pierce's friends and their stupid antics. I knew it was them who suggested trashing a random boat and that he was only forcing me to go because he felt I was cooped up in our apartment too much.

It wasn't that I was anti-social or anything but I just wasn't a big fan of going clubbing or getting high in the alleys. To me it seemed tiring doing all these things in a constant circle. I would much rather while away my time on the studying or watching my favourite series on Pierce's Netflix account (lord knows it's so much more fun that way) or just surf the net and chat with some of my friends back home.

I sighed decided to give my Philosophy textbook a little break seeing as I wasn't sure if it was safe to touch after all the damage Pierce inflicted on it. The stupid fucker didn't even realize I got this from the library.

Oh well, maybe a bit of fresh air would be good for my knowledge saddled brain.

Who knows?

I shivered mentally scolding myself for listening to Pierce when he said it wasn't so cold outside. Actually, I mentally kicked myself for listening to him when he said it would get warmer when I wanted to go back inside to get a thicker jacket instead of my thin little hoodie. Come to think of it, I might be covered in a lot of bruises if I had to hit myself for every time I listened to Pierce's suggestions.

"Could you tell your roommate to hurry the hell up?!" one of Pierce's obnoxious friends by the name of Jerry called out.

I rolled my eyes from inside the car fumbling to get out. It wasn't like I'd wanted to come out here in the first place I thought shooting Pierce a look to which he sheepishly sent me another apologetic look.

"I have a name you know." I mumbled loud enough to Jerry's hearing and walked past him before he could make any other comment. It was no mystery that I didn't like him that much and I knew the feeling was mutual also. He was the kind of guy who was into banging a differently girl every week for the fun of it which didn't sit so well with me.

Not because I was gay, but felt women deserved to be respected because they were also humans and in some aspects better than men. I was raised by a strong woman so I would know.

The other two guys Mario and Isaac just glanced at me but didn't say anything else as I leaned on the hood of the Jeep. They were in the same alley as him but didn't talk much about my presence so I just let it slide.

"You ok mate?" another voice called out behind me as I stood by the car. It was James one of Pierce's other friends who I could stand a lot better.

"Yeah it's just so freaking cold out here. Who even came up with this pissy idea?" I huffed out loud.

He laughed that sweet husky laugh of his "Hey, at least it's out of the box. Getting high on an expensive boat seems like one of those bucket list kinds of things." James and Pierce were the only ones who knew I was gay out of the five guys. Pierce was bi as you've guessed so it really wasn't a big deal to him.

But James was surprisingly cool about it and didn't judge me in any way. Maybe that was why my humongous crush on him got bigger. It almost seemed pathetic, I was in college and apparently too old to have crushes but the thing with James is that he was cool and easy to get along with. Not to mention a terrific listener.

But the tragedy was he was also as straight as they came.

"That's just some stupid blind expectation people make when they don't wanna convince themselves about how boring their life is." I stated surveying the marina. It was a good hour away from where the university and our apartment since it was only a ten minute walk from each other.

Normally in the day it was beautiful when the sun was out and you could actually go to the seafront bar. There were hundreds of boats floating around so I wondered which one we were going to be gracing this evening.

"Well making one shows that they already know don't you think?" James asked with a knowing grin. I decided to give him a playful shove the way a bro would do but ignored the way my heart clenched.

"We gotta be careful in case the watchman's here." Pierce said cautiously for a moment but Jerry patted his shoulder. "Relax; it'll be a piece of cake dude."

He smirked at me to let me know that he had been taunting me as if it wasn't already obvious. I rolled my eyes shoving my hands into my pockets. I glanced carelessly at all the boats but stopped when I spotted one in particular that made my eyes widen.

Holy cow. It looked at least forty feet with two sleek white hulls, a deck, a roomy cabin, and towering over a tall mast. I was no real expert on boats but there was no denying that this one was a beauty. I peeked at the name on the side The Silver Phoenix. Hmm definitely a special one.

"How about this one?" I pointed bringing their attention towards it. Pierce whistled lowly; "I don't know. It seems to fancy." Jerry complained not even glancing at me.

"Come on mate that's the point of this whole thing. Or you want us to take some shitty blow-up boat?" James tried to persuade him.

Jerry looked hard and I could see he wanted to get on. Probably would have done so if he had been the first to spot it and not me.

He sighed "Fine."

Mario and Isaac just shrugged like they did every time Jerry approved something.

James patted me on the back before walking up cautiously to the dock with me behind him. We all had to make do without a gangplank seeing as it wasn't our boat. There was still the part of me that didn't want to do this, but I couldn't back out now seeing as I was the one who picked the boat and made everyone else get on.

I almost slipped when it was my turn but James managed to help my before I fell into the cold slimy water.

"I've got you." he smiled pulling me up.

"Thanks." I breathed.

"There goes Humpty Dumpty." Jerry commented in what sounded like contempt. At least Pierce managed to save my dignity by giving him a scolding nudge.

Any fear or doubts I had about doing this completely evaporated once I saw how it looked. The deck had a rigid canopy over it and to the side was a table and a U shaped banquette covered in ox blood coloured leather and looked like it could seat at least 7 people. Plus there was a glass door that led way to an interior that I'm sure was as sick as the rest of this boat.

The only thing I gathered was that whoever owned this boat had a lot of money to throw around. And apparently the right way.

"This is swanky." Pierce commented looking excited again before going to explore the rest of the boat.

"Let's get the party started." James rubbed his hands together before bringing out his precious stash of weed. He rolled it, lit it up and took a long drag before handing it over to me to do the same. I had smoked with the guys a few times before managed to back out before I was completely stoned out of my mind.

It was also because I didn't like hanging with them when they were high because that seemed to make them a lot more crazier and irrational than normal, especially Jerry. Him sober was already tearing me down well enough.

"Don't hog it all." Jerry snatched the joint right out of my hands even though I had barely taken a drag.

"Hey we have enough to go round." James scolded him earning a mental praise from me.

There was a thudding sound that made my heart skip a beat but I relaxed as soon as I saw that it was just Pierce with an unusually cocky grin.

"Look what I found." He brought out an expensive looking bottle from behind him.

"Shit Pierce nobody said anything about stealing!" I whispered yelled at him.

Mario grabbed the bottle "Relax princess we're just having a little fun." It was the first thing he said all night.

"There was a lot more in the back. It probably even won't be noticed." Pierce replied with added confidence and I hadn't even seen him take any weed yet.

They popped the bottle of wine while giggling like schoolgirls and took turns taking swigs like it was their last. I declined because I didn't plan on getting high out of my mind like the rest of them and there was still this nagging feeling at the back of my mind.

No matter how beautiful we were still on someone else's yacht, without permission.

I wasn't so morally uptight but I did know when something was every shade of fucked up, even for crazy pranks.

"You ok man?" James asked suddenly noticing my sullen state.

I nodded "Yeah."

After an hour of joint smoking, drinking and singing terrible ballads, the guys managed to pile themselves out of the boat surprisingly without falling into the water. With my help of course. My head was pounding and it was 3 AM already. So far all of the fun Pierce promised me wasn't true but at least this time I didn't get into any trouble.

"Shit I think I forgot my jacket." I announced in the Jeep once we had driven a safe distance from the marina.

"Can you be anymore dumb Ross?" Jerry groaned.

I narrowed my eyes at him "I'm sorry I forgot it hauling your stupid ass on the docks."

"You fucking arse-"

"Hey stop it guys." Pierce said managing to form a sentence despite his half stoned state. "Just hurry up man."

"Yeah. Whatever." I slammed the door after getting out of the car. Jerry said something but I didn't hear it and thought it was probably best that way.

I managed to climb onto the boat and spotted my jacket immediately. Before going off I took a look around the yacht thinking to myself about how this beauty was almost worth it all. I've never been one to covet things from other people because I was raised believing that as long as you were comfortable fancy things didn't matter.

But I couldn't help feeling a pang of envy towards whoever owned this boat.

"Who the hell are you?!" a loud masculine voice sent me straight from my thoughts and drained all the blood in my face.

Oh shit, guess I spoke too soon.

Chapter 2 - So It Begins.......

In case of any inaccuracies I don't live in London full time. I only visit a lot and I'm not aquainted with their schooling system. Anyways I'll stop yapping and let you get to the reading

P.S unedited so sorry for any mistakes

The fear was crippling. Like my mind was telling me to run like a deer but my body had completely shut down and refused to make a single move, betraying me totally. The ultimate betrayal actually.

"Why the fuck are you on my boat?!" the voice snapped something in me again.

"I-I"- started to say but got cut short when I felt two large hands grab me from behind and yank me up earning a shout from me. It was another guy super buffed with an etched scowl on his face that clearly showed he was ready to tear me head off my shoulders.

"Hey don't kill him yet Timothy." The voice said again but much calmer than before. It was then that I managed to look up and see who was talking.

There was a guy standing by the glass doors with a series of mixed expressions on his face. Mostly anger, but there seemed to be a hint of what looked like curiosity. He walked closer and I noticed that he was barefoot but it didn't seem awkward at all. I noticed that he was wearing a loose-fitting shirt with regular jeans and his hair was a tousled brunette that I would have dared call attractive if it wasn't for the situation.

"What's your name?" he said so smoothly I blinked. My heart was pounding like a bitch from fear so you couldn't really judge my reaction.

"K-Kendall Ross." I barely stuttered out. He cocked his head to the side and that's when I noticed that he couldn't have been much older than me, but probably mid-twenties or so. He also had a surprisingly posh accent but I didn't let my mind dwell on that.

He hummed "Well Kendall if you don't want my good friend Timothy here to snap your neck and toss you into the water I suggest you tell me why you're in my yacht."

Timothy's grip tightened on my neck making the words spill out faster "My friends and I were just doing some stupid dare but I swear we didn't trash or steal anything." The way I blabbered didn't seem to make much sense but the guy must have understood at least a little bit because he nodded his head.

"I know you don't know me but I'm sure you can tell that I don't like being lied to." He calmly moving closer to me and I couldn't help but shiver. He was threatening me but somehow my stupid body had decided to come up with a different reaction. God this is worse than Stockholm syndrome.

"Seriously dude I'm not lying! It was stupid and dumb but they just thought it was funny to trash some random boat and get high, that's all. I was just dragged along." This time my voice was a lot clearer so I hoped that he would believe me. My voice was already going higher than the manly standards.

"So where are they now?" he asked after a while.

I glanced around "Probably gone now. I forgot my jacket so I came back." I held up my diesel hoodie as proof.

The guy was silent for some time, most likely processing my story and wondering whether to believe me or not. I hoped he did believe me with every fibre of being within me because this was not in any way my fault.

It was Pierce and his stupid convincing skills.

"Drop him." He said after an eternity and suddenly I was dropped quickly onto the hard deck floor. I groaned from the pain in my back but hopefully this remained as a sign that he might believe me.

"Thank you Timothy." He nodded. The burly guy took that as a sign to leave by casting me a hard look like he still didn't believe my story even though I was being honest.

"You sure Axel?" he asked one more time but he still nodded. Axel, finally there was a name to the face. If I was honest he kind of did strike me as an Axel. The burly guy left probably to the other side of the yacht probably to check if there were any other dumb college kids. Leaving me alone under the piercing gaze of the guy I presumed was called Axel.

I was about to stand up but he crouched in front of me carefully placing his hand on the nape of my neck before forcing me to face him eye to eye. I would be lying if I said the gesture didn't both scare me and leave me breathless at the same time. At the same time I got a peek of his collarbone which had what seemed to be a large tattoo inked but it was a little too dark to tell.

His scent clouded my brain even though I recognized that it was Armani, from the time Pierce got a sample bottle from the store where he worked. Even then it didn't smell as rough or spicy or completely alluring.

Maybe it just had to do with the wearer.

"Now you must have gathered that I'm a lot nicer than Timothy over there." He said gently caressing my nape which felt wrong and hot at the same time. Shit, this was a stranger and one ready to kill me for trashing his boat no doubt. I nodded solemnly so he continued.

"Which is why I'm giving you one last chance to be honest with me: did someone send you here?" Axel asked me one more time. What was it with this guy? I told him the complete gospel truth and he still didn't believe me.

"Dude I told you"-

"Don't call me dude." His grip on my neck had tightened and I tried not to gasp in pain. His tone was darker and less patient with me now.

"I told you, I'm not lying. Nobody sent me here. We just picked this boat on random not like we knew it was yours. I'm not lying." My voice was shaky but tried to make it as honest possible. "Besides you could beat me up and I would still say the same thing."

Axel's, if I could call him that, expression remained the same all the while I talked.

"Ok kid. I believe you." his grip dropped on my neck and I sighed in immediate relief. I rubbed it to avail some of the pain because I'm sure there must have been a large handprint there judging by how hard he had held me.

"I'm so sorry and I can promise that you'll never see me again." I assured him managing to stand up on my own feet.

"But if you are lying to me I will find you and the end result won't be very pleasant." From the shade his eyes took it didn't take much for me to know that he was very serious on carrying in out his threat.

I gulped "Like I said; I'm not lying to you. It was just a stupid prank I swear on my unborn children."

"Hmm." He mused. I stood there for a little bit not really sure what to do next. "I should probably go now. And I promise again that this will never happen again."

"Don't promise." He said and I couldn't help but wonder if it had any double meaning.

I was completely tired once I got back to my apartment. The living room lights were off meaning Pierce was asleep annoying me further than I already was. We made an agreement that when anyone one of us was out for the night the other would leave the lights on as a considerate gesture. The rule was created mostly for Pierce's benefit seeing as he was out a lot more than me and the poor guy had the tendency to knock things over in the dark.

That was partly why I was so pissed off because I tried to always look out for Pierce in everything I did but he couldn't even be bothered to leaving the freaking lights on after him and his friends abandoned me to my fate on the yacht.

It was almost seven and I had a morning lecture which would take me at least 45 minutes to get to. I groaned taking off my jacket because I was still beyond tired from the weed and it wasn't so much fun walking from the marina for 20 minutes before I could get a bus to the apartment complex. It was my sheer luck some graceful deity had prompted me to put my London bus card in my wallet the day before.

"Kendall? That you?" I cursed on hearing Pierce's voice.

He appeared wearing nothing but a pair of basketball shorts clearly too big for him judging by how low they rode on his hips.

"You're back?" he asked rubbing his eyes as if he were really surprised.

"Nah this is just a figment of your imagination standing in our kitchen." The sarcasm in my voice was hard enough to knock a horse over.

"Sorry for leaving you back there- it's just that I was so wired and Jerry said you weren't coming back-"

I slammed the cupboard a little harder than necessary. Of course Jerry had to be involved. It would be a fucking field day if that son of a lowlife wasn't involved in anything that caused my demise. I went to the fridge to grab some juice completely ignoring Pierce.

"I know it's not an excuse mate but all the guys were asleep and trashed like me so we couldn't really function much 'cause Jerry was driving." He apologized and I snorted pouring my orange juice.

"It's no big deal. It's not like I had to walk back, at the crack ass of dawn." I gave him a bitter smile before downing my juice. By now Pierce's expression resembled that of a kicked puppy and that was one look I ALWAYS tried to avoid. He was a pretty sensitive fellow so it didn't take much to make him sad or touchy feeling. Even now I tried to push the urge to hug him at the back of my mind and remain with my emotionless façade.

I had every right to be angry at him.

"I'm really sorry Kendall that was a shit move and makes me a shit friend." Oh no only sincere Pierce ever called me by my full name instead of Kenny.

I sighed and hugged him against my will even though it totally felt right. My mom used to tell me that I get easily manipulated by people's emotional displays but it wasn't my fault that I couldn't stand it when people around me were sad.

"It's not fine, but I can't stay mad at you forever P." I said hesitantly pulling away. "Just don't pull any shitty moves again?"

He nodded furiously "Total shit move, so shitty it deserves to be flushed down a toilet."

My face contorted in disgust "Ok that's overboard now." I ruffled his hair and he playfully swatted my hand. "At least you didn't get in trouble."

I tensed at the phrase but brushed it off "Nah I didn't." if I let him know about my incident on the boat with Axel and Mr. Meaty it would have egged on his guilt. As satisfying as it sounded, I wasn't a heartless guy and Pierce already seemed sorry enough. Now if there was anybody I would like to skull-smash into a wall Jerry seemed like the perfect choice.......

"Mate I think you really need to shower now." Pierce said pointing to his phone and making my eyes widen. "Shit!"

"You ok for lunch?" he asked and I nodded quickly rushing to my room to grab my stuff before showering.

"Here." Pierce offered me a 10 pound note. A slow grin spread to my face as I snatched it "All is forgiven my wonderful and sexy roommate." He scoffed flipping me off before leaving to do whatever. I wasn't mad anymore, but who the hell says no to 10 quid?

Thankful to deity I only had two lectures which were pretty short so that left me enough time to browse through my favourite coffee shop Steamers for a quick lunch. Settled with my caramel frap and a delicious salmon and egg sandwich, I took out my laptop mindlessly browsing through some of my notes for the day and took advantage of the coffee shop's Wi-Fi to send a quick e-mail to my mom and step father.

"Hi Kenny!" a familiar high pitched voice squealed making me groaned silently. Clarissa Downers waltzed to my table happy that she had finally caught me and I wished I sat inside today. She was wearing a short green sleeveless dress that made me uncomfortable seeing as it was a very windy day.

The problem I had with this girl is that she never managed to get it in her skull that I was gay. Nope she took every moment to try and 'seduce' me into going out with her. Several times I tried to tell her that we could be friends but it only seemed like my words went through one ear and came out another as if she had fresh air, instead of a brain, in her skull.

Her last name really did her justice. Downer.

"I'm busy Clarissa." I tried but she invited herself to my table smiling brightly.

"Hi Kenny! Damn you look superhot today." Clarissa purred but it was deeply disturbing. I closed my laptop "Not now. Please find some other poor queer to torment." Gosh didn't she have any friends to force her to go shopping or something? Maybe her friends were just as wacked in the head as her.

"Huh?" She looked confused, as if what I said really didn't make sense to her pretty little head. "But I wanted to see you."

I rolled my eyes "Look Clarissa you're a sweet girl but I'm not into you. I've told you I'm gay, g-a-y. Into long sticks not sticky pools, queer, batting for the other team. Taking the other side of the highway. I vote for twinks not titties."

I had used every single homosexual metaphor I could think of, even the deeply weird ones. In fact the lady beside me had an expression mixed with confusion and laughter. Not that I really blamed her anyway. Clarissa flicked her red hair with her glitter blue nails "That's just what you think. Just have a go with me and I promise you'll understand that you can't be gay. We're meant to be together Kenny."

I give up.

I just grabbed my messenger bag and stuff from my table without a single word despite her protests.

"Kenny where are you going?!"

"Far away from your psychotic ass!" I shouted without looking back. I could hear the little heels of her shoes getting closer so I walked faster not minding if I got hit by a bus. Death by the London transport system was better than this. Hell the incident on the yacht this morning was WAY better than this.

That girl needed to be sent to a home.

After 20 minutes I didn't hear anymore shouts of "Kenny love!" so it was safe to assume I lost her. My apartment complex was in sight so I walked up the stairs instead of taking the elevator since it had a tendency of taking too much time and needed to be fixed.

By the time I got to my apartment Pierce was in the kitchen with a box. "Hey P."

"Hey Kendall something came in the mail for you." Pierce replied holding a crème coloured box with a blue ribbon. I frowned dropping my bag on the couch "A package? I didn't expect any packages today."

"Well did you order anything online?" he asked him and I replied with a look that clearly said "Stupid question P".

My mom only sent me sweaters and knit scarfs towards winter and there weren't any other relatives who sent me presents randomly. I opened the box to see a fairly small velvet box.

"What if it's a bomb mate?" Pierce joked.

"You watch too many movies man." I told him thoughtlessly curious as to what was in the box. I cracked it carefully, before slowly opening a box to see what was inside. My mouth dropped instantly.

"Mate is that a fucking watch?" He asked stunned.

"Well what does it look like?" I managed to reply wittily even though I was still in awe myself. No it wasn't just any ordinary watch. It was a freaking Rolex, one of the latest models I remembered some of the boys in my World Literature class going on about. It was so new and sparkly that I was afraid to touch it.

Pierce whistled "What kind of friends have you been keeping?"

"I dunno who could have sent this." I said honestly dropping the watch on the counter. There was literally no one I knew alive that had this kind of money to spend on a watch for a little 19 year old me.

"There's a note in the box." He observed handing it over to me. It was written in one of those fancy cursives that you couldn't help but feel jealous at every time you read them.

Dear Kendall,

I hope this little present makes up for our unfortunate fiasco

A.Gold

"Who on God's earth is A.Gold?" Pierce all but whispered to me. A gut wrenching feeling stirred in my stomach but I couldn't figure it out.

"I don't know dude."

Picture to the side is the watch---------->

Chapter 3 - Cocktails and Four Wheelers

I'm so nervous about this chapter but I hope it turns out great. I'm glad this story is getting great feedback and I'm happy. This dedication goes to the person above because I fangirled when she added this story to her reading list ;)

Ok.......Shutting up now.

Red Velvet was a relatively new club, but for some reason it had become one of the most popular amongst the university students. Maybe because of its most popular DJ, Spinderella. Yes it was a techy kind of name but she was a female DJ and apparently super good from what I'd heard. Also very popular with all of the guys.

And of course Pierce had managed to convince me that it was the best idea to tag along with him on a fine Friday night......as usual. We were only going alone which was fine with me because I was pretty sure that the next time I say Jerry I would beat him with a frying pan for that stupid stunt two days ago.

"I am so ready to get wasted." Pierce all but moaned as he styled his hair into its signature quiff. I rolled my eyes spritzing on some cologne "Please, the sun sets and you're ready to get wasted." He's Irish so it's in his blood to gulp alcohol like its water. It's a complete mystery as to why he's so light-weight though.

"You my friend, need to get laid." Pierce patted me on the shoulder with a too sweet smile.

I scoffed glancing in the mirror "I'm sorry bro; unlike you I don't meet many people happy to do the dance with no pants on the first date."

He rolled his eyes as soon as he realized what I was implying "There is a fine line between being slutty and easy-going-"

"They're the fucking same thing dude." I stated for him. He huffed leaving the bathroom "Insult me all you want I was only trying to help. Don't come running to me when you're forty and your dick has shrivelled up due to no action."

"Not if yours fall off first due to overuse." I said bemused at Pierce and his theatrics. Sometimes I wondered why he wasn't studying Drama; he clearly had the knack for it. But alas he was wasting his time with Criminology even though he was clearly good at it. Satisfied with my appearance I strolled back to my room to see Pierce cradling my watch which was supposed to be placed securely in my bedside drawer.

"What the fuck?! Don't touch my stuff Pierce!" I snatched it from his claws and he immediately raised up his hands in surrender.

"Sorry." He apologized in a very small voice.

I frowned "We don't know who sent it so I appreciate you not touching it until we do." I looked down at the watch and admired its tiny little stones before placing it back in the box.

"Come on Kendall!" he whined "It's probably some rich long lost relative who's discovered you and thinks you're good-looking as to grace you with a watch so there!"

Sometimes I wonder how Pierce gets those distinctions of his because his reasoning does unspeakable things to me.

"That doesn't even make sense."

"That thing is priceless! Maybe we should sell it and buy ourselves a convertible!" He suggested excitedly sounding very serious.

I shook of the urge to say something mean "By tomorrow I'm going down to the post office to see if I can find out the address of whoever sent it." I tried sounding patient. "So no touching it till then."

"No touching?" He put on his cute puppy face.

My lips twitched but I forced the smile away "Absolutely none P."

"Not even if it's by your awesome roommate with an amazing ass?"

Sometimes I wish I could sell him on eBay already............

One of the things I loved about living in England was the fact that 18 was the age limit. There some states, like in Cali where I'm from, that only allow you to drink or go clubbing from 21. I was already 19 which gave me the green light but sometimes I liked to carry my other ID which said I was 20 but only because there were clubs a bit weary to adolescents with the 1 digit attached to their ages.

But this wasn't one of those clubs and I was glad.

We were bombarded with sweaty bodies and Usher's 'Scream' as soon as we came in, automatically bringing out the party animal in Pierce.

"Let's go get some drinks!" He suggested grabbing my hands and pulling me towards the bar. The bartender was a very attractive man but not really my type.

"Hey Rod!" Pierce piped up.

Rod grinned throwing his signature hand towel over his shoulder "What can I get you boys tonight?"

"I'll have a Bloody Mary." I said.

He turned to Pierce "I'll have a Dirty Martini."

"Well how dirty do you want it?" he asked.

Pierce smirked that alluring smirk of his "Well make it filthy." Rod winked at him before going off to get our drinks. He may claim bisexual all he wants, but Pierce is obviously as flaming as they come. I've never seen him hook up with a girl though he claims that he's been with plenty before he met me. But in all honesty I've never seen Pierce eye up a girl that way, even when they flirted openly with him. He used to say that he never really found anyone worthwhile but even a blind man could see that he wasn't into them.

In my opinion he only said he was bi so his parents would get off his case and hope that one day he would bring a nice girl. Hell would turn into Antarctica before that happened. But part of me wished he would stop living in self-denial just to please his parents.

"Here you go pretty boys." Rod came back with our drinks and an extra sultry smile especially for Pierce. Someone was going to bump and grind in the back room soon.

I rolled my eyes focusing on my Bloody Mary.

DJ Spinderella turned out to be as good as everyone claimed because I was seriously impressed. She was a short pixie like girl with short red hair covered with her large headphones. She was seriously fast also throwing me off with her skills. It was no wonder she had gotten really popular in the club scene.

"Let's dance Kenny!" Pierce screeched obviously buzzed from his two drinks. I shook my head "Nah, you go fun I'll sit this one out."

He pouted but got over it and skipped to the dance floor where I could already see two guys eyeing him up.

"Can I get a shot?" I asked Rod who nodded.

I downed three shots of vodka within two minutes and felt as though my skin buzzed alive instantly. I'm not the kind of person to drink without limits but tonight I felt like letting myself go for some reason. Uni was stressful as usual, coupled with the fact that I also had some very important decisions to make. I also missed my mom and found myself dialling her number a few times the previous week but decided against it. If I called her I would let out everything that was troubling me instantly and I had promised her before leaving that I would be able handle being alone. I didn't need to disappoint her now.

"Excuse me are you Kendall Ross?" a tall man asked me.

"Yes that's me."

"Could you come with me for a little bit?" he more like stated instead asked.

I blinked "Why?"

He curved his lip "You'll find out don't worry." It was a serious gamble but I downed my drink and followed feeling a bit tense.

We went through the back reliving me immensely as the front was crowded with too many people. The cold night hit me as he directed me towards a black SUV. He opened the door and it took me a few seconds to realize that I was supposed to enter.

I said a silent prayer hoping that I didn't make a mistake. I sat on the plush leather seats holding my breath.

"Hello Kendall." A familiar deep voice said sending tingles down my spine. I turned to my side feeling my heart drop a thousand kilometres down my chest. It was the guy from the boat.

It was Axel.

Am I dead?

Dear lord I'm dead.

Is this death?

It must be death.

And he looked hot. Shit, apparently my hormones can't stop misbehaving in the face of danger. I thought he believed me about the boat incident? Maybe he found one of his bottles missing and came back to finish me off. God my ghost is so going to give Pierce a proper beat down, the drunken fucker.

"Relax I'm not going to slash your throat." He said sounding amused. My current fearful state must have been amusing to him.

"W-What do you want with me?" I asked ashamed at how small my voice was. He leaned closer and DAMN that scent. At least I smelt something good before I died.

"Did you like the watch I sent you?" he asked and my face scrunched in confusion.

"Wait that was you? But it said A. Gold-" I shut up when it clicked.

Oh.

He smirked "Axel Gold." As if he was introducing himself for the first time. I can't believe I didn't figure it sooner, but excuse me for not expecting a guy whose boat I crashed to send me a thousand dollar watch the next day.

"Don't think I'm not grateful, but why did you send me a watch Mr. Gold?" I asked swallowing the last word.

He scoffed "Call me Axel. I'm older than you but not by much please." Hmm then definitely within the late twenties age bracket. "And gifts can be sent as a form of appreciation you know."

"I don't recall anything I did requiring you appreciation." I stated.

Axel smiled and dear lord I could say it was slow, dark and delicious to watch. My body shifted uncomfortably because it suddenly felt hot in the four-wheeler. He stroked the side of my face "But I appreciate you Kendall, very much."

My breathing was erratic "What do you want from me Axel?"

He moved closer allowing his white shirt and expose a bit of delicious inked skin like I remembered. It was surprising that someone like him could have a tattoo. It only made him a lot more appealing in my eyes.

"Everything. Everything you can give me Kendall. Just be short I want you."

Was I hearing right? This gorgeous man had suddenly decided that I was some prized porcelain he wanted in his collection? This was going too Fifty Shades of Grey for me.

"Are you gay?" I blurted out.

Axel wet his lips before answering "Let's just say, when I want something I don't let gender stop me."

"So you're gay." I deadpanned earning a chuckle from him. "Yes." He replied simply. This was surreal. I wasn't some object someone could want and toss when they were bored no matter how stunning or gorgeous he seemed.

"Sorry but I'm not an object so you can't want me." I apologized my stubborn and rational side coming out again. Axel simply nodded like I was a toddler making an attempt at something grown up "I understand. But hasn't it crossed you mind how I knew where to find you?"

Wait, how did he know where to find me?

"I saw you by chance. You were trying to get into the club with a particularly loud boy next to you and so I pulled over." perfect description of you-know-who.

"You're American, 19 years old, you're an English major also minoring in Art. You've been living with a roommate and you have been for a year. Should I go on?" he knew my address which obvious seeing as he sent me a parcel two days before.

I blinked "Before you say anything I did a brief check on you and made sure that you weren't lying about being on my yacht." Ok I still took some offence to that one. "You're quite an interesting fellow, which only makes me want to claim you more."

"And what if I don't want to be claimed?" I retorted.

He grinned grabbing my palm and pressing a light kiss that seemed to have more effect on me than 20 bottles of alcohol "Are you sure?"

Oh no. I didn't want to pathetically puddle in my jeans just because of his voice. I wouldn't be subjected to that kind of behaviour. Slutty reactions were Pierce's thing not mine.

Axel placed his hand on the nape of my neck like last time but this time I was afraid for a completely differently reason. I breathed in his Armani as he brought his lips to my exposed collarbone sucking the skin and causing a gasp to escape from my lips. If this was death then I say a fucking sayonara to the world.

"Do you want me Kendall?" he hummed into my neck. My fingers trembled "God-"

"Answer me."

"Yes, God yes I do." I almost pleaded. My brain's function seemed to have shut off for the moment and didn't have any interest in coming back on. Axel bit roughly surely leaving a visible mark making my eyes shut instantly. It felt too good to ignore.

"Fuck." I groaned inwardly. He hummed continuing his actions on the spot above my collarbone. "Delicious." Before pulling away abruptly.

"So, what will it be Kendall?" he asked looking as calm as ever while I was utterly wrecked. I was breathing hard "I'm not signing any contracts am I?"

"No but I will take your word and hold you firmly by it." Axel replied. "And by saying yes you'll be agreeing to be with me." It sounded too abrupt, like a sentence. Not really a death sentence or such but I had a feeling it would be a very long lasting agreement. Very long.

And I wasn't sure if I was ready for something like that.

"You don't even know me and I have no freaking idea who you are." I said looking down at the seats. It was true; up until a few days I had no idea who he was. If it wasn't for the incident on his yacht he wouldn't have known me either.

"But I want to. Please." He caressed my cheek.

Maybe I was selling my soul to the devil at this point but I was drawn completely to him already. I sighed "Ok." There it was a stamp in my fate. Only the heavens knew what would happen now.

"Hand me your phone." I did wearily "8920."

He immediately typed something I couldn't see then handed it back to me so I could see that it was his number saved as Axel.

"I'll see you tomorrow." Axel said as I gripped my phone. "And wear your watch."

"Ok." I replied and he sent me a small wisp of a smile. "But I'm not agreeing to anything yet. I just want to know you like you said."

He nodded "Noted."

My life was about to take an interesting turn.

The yummy, er, wonderful Andre Hamann as Axel Gold to the side (or above if youre using the app)

Chapter 4 - Juggling Memories

I feel like I've been updating frequently........Anyways I hope whoever reads this chapter is ok with it. There's some angst if you squint well enough. Enjoy the song to the side 'cause I happen to love it lots and think it goes with the chapter....kind of *awkward nod*

P.S My chapters have been long so I'm thinking of making them shorter but not too short

Oh. My. Gosh. What have I done?! I stared at the ceiling in my room clutching the duvet so hard my knuckles were beginning to turn white. I was contemplating on whether I had imagined what happened during the last 8 hours or it was real. Like really real.

I seriously doubt that I let a man who threatened me not long ago fondle me so closely in the back seat of his car and tell me that he wanted me like it was the most natural thing in the world. Not forgetting the fact that I melted like a pudding in a cup every time he touched me. Just remembering made me scream into my pillow like an annoyed preteen girl. Not just because I couldn't believe it, but because I darn well liked it.

The human nature is so screwed up.

I eyed the watch warily deciding whether I should wear it or not. Come to think of it where the hell was I wearing it to? Axel never told me where or when we were going to meet up. All he said was that he would see me today without actually disclosing the time or location.

Gah, it was completely frustrating. Not because I wanted to see him, but because in the short time I'd known him he had managed to make me mushy and confused and bewildered all at the same time with just single a twitch of his eyebrow. I didn't even know the man to begin with.

"Urgh you look worse than me and I had a lot more drinks." Pierce observed standing at my door. I rolled my eyes covering myself with the duvet "I know and I resent you for it."

He chuckled "Well you can blame my genes then."

He had no idea about what I was up to last night which was fine with me. Although I'm pretty sure I was the last thing on his when he was banging Rod the bartender in the back room.

"I'm tired and irritated so please go away." I muttered with my duvet still over my head. Pierce raised up his hands in surrender "Ok sleepy beauty. See you when I get back."

I mumbled something incoherent.

"And I'll make dinner tonight."

An unconscious smile found its way to my face because as weird and annoying as Pierce is, cooking is one of his many strange and hidden talents. I was a pretty decent cook but I'm only narrowed to a few memorized recipes unlike him.

"Bye! I'm out!" He announced before he front door slammed shut. Last night I left him at Red Velvet and took the bus back home but he got a ride with one of the guys at the club. I felt guilty but he didn't seem to mind at all. When I thought about it hard enough it was probably because he still felt bad about leaving me at the marina.

That must mean we're even now.

I sighed eventually getting up from the warm mushy bed that seemed to be the only comforting thing in my life right now. I didn't have any lecture today since it was Saturday and was a total god-send but I still needed to go to the library and get some research done. But that wasn't until much later today giving me enough to laze around and pool in my thoughts all morning.

My phone was on the bedside drawer and it took me a while to remember that Axel had typed in his phone number before I left. Did he want me to call him? Was that it? I stared at the phone for a little longer before deciding that if he needed to talk to me, he would find some way to do so. After all he had negotiated this whole crazy encounter. Satisfied with myself I went into the bathroom to brush and shower then proceeded to make myself a light breakfast.

Though I cursed thoroughly when I realized that those ghastly red marks were still on my neck, making me madder and more turned on than ever.

While I was stirring my coffee my phone rang and immediately I shuddered thinking it was Axel. But it only turned out to be Mara my sister calling from the States. A sense of dread enveloped me; what did she want? My mother had probably persuaded her to seeing as I was her little brother and we hadn't seen for quite some time. That was the only reason she would call me. Along with some other reasons I wouldn't like to mention.

"Shit." I murmured taking a huge sip of my coffee. "I can't take this."

So I dropped my phone on the couch muffled by some pillows so that the ringing wouldn't make too much noise. Yes I know it seemed cruel ignoring my older sister's call but there were some things better left unsaid and forgotten. My sister and I had so much history and it wasn't in the normal sibling rivalry way.

Mara was about 6 years my senior trying to complete her Master's in Business in Colombia at the moment. Beautiful and always articulate there was nobody who wouldn't love her company at first sight. The smartest one in our family that got all the praise from our extended family meanwhile it was still taking everybody time to adjust their heads around that fact that I was gay. Only my mother seemed to be ok with it.

I smiled bitterly as I drank my coffee and ignored the ringing phone.

"Hi Kendall!" a voice startled me as I was currently typing a 3000 word essay for my professor. It was James with that stomach flipping smile of his making his way to my table. "Fancy bumping into you here. Is it alright if I sit?"

"Sure." I moved some of my stuff away so that he could place his while also trying to hide my blush.

He placed his backpack on the floor beside his chair and dropped some of his textbooks on the table.

"Sorry I've been cranky these past few days. I'm submitting this report that's supposed be like 30% of my grade." He apologized due to the number of books he had.

"It's fine." I smiled. "This is university anyway."

James chuckled "Half the time I wonder if I should just drop out. But my folks would kill me if I quote "throw my future away" like really." I could sense some resentment in his tone but decided not to address it. Back in my senior year I remember my mom telling me that she would never force me to go to college or do anything that would make me feel miserable but she wanted the best for me and thought that university was it.

I knew it was though, just not close to home. At first she was heartbroken with my choice to school so far away but got over it once I assured her that it was what I wanted. It of course didn't tell her that there were other things I was tired of facing at home and decided that somewhere far away was what I needed to cling back to that state of sanity I once held. Although I wasn't sure it would ever really be that simple.

"Kendall!"

"Huh?" I snapped out of my thoughts to see James' amused expression. "I was asking you have any plans today."

"Sorry I blanked out there. Not but I'm not really in the mood to do anything. Maybe just curl in front of the TV and indulge myself in several Netflix series." I explained with a brief smile.

James nodded "Pity though. I was hoping if you wanted to hang out or something with me. I know I only see you when I'm hanging out with Pierce and Jerry but I wanted us to just hang out together. Y'know as mates."

His voice was calm but little did he know that my heart was pumping enough blood for the whole of Africa in my chest. James wanted to hang out with me. It almost seemed too good to be true. His phone rang ruining the moment but he whipped it out and scoffed at the ID before dropping it.

"Why don't you want to pick it?" I asked curiously.

"It's just my girlfriend Stephanie." He said nonchalantly. I tried not to let my disappointment show. I mean, of course I knew he was straight all this time but I had no idea that he was in a relationship. That only made my crush on him feel wrong in a way, like it was intruding. Of course he was taken.

"You guys fighting?" I tried to smirk nonchalantly.

James shook his head "She's been getting too clingy lately. I mean I like to go out and not tell her where I am every waking second. Like it's just so fucking suffocating mate."

I shrugged a shoulder "Most girls are like that dude. I mean it's normal for her to want to be around you all the time, you're her boyfriend."

He snorted "Fuck I am. This is Uni for Pete's sake, sometimes I wanna party and go out and not have to report to her always. We're not engaged or anything. Girls are just too clingy, you know?"

"No I don't." I murmured facing my laptop and thereby signalling the end of our conversation. I didn't to stop feeling a wounded animal about this. James was straight; he'd always been straight and will continue to be straight until a meteor decides to hit earth so there was no need sulking over something I'd never have in the first place.

Yes he did have perfect hair and toned body I had accidentally discovered when Pierce dragged me for a pool party once. Maybe his smile was the essence of human life and his dimples were to kill for. Sure he was a great guy and we talked a lot about stuff we had in common but he was also going to be that guy in college. Just another person who occupied my thoughts during my tertiary education but there was no long run thing.

He didn't even like me that way.

So the best thing was to forget all about him and gracefully accept my everlasting promotion into the friend zone. I had decided within myself and that was good enough. I turned to look at the library clock and noticed him reading intently about something in his Gothic Architecture book, eyebrows all scrunched up adorably.

But there was no way I ever stop admiring his looks.

My cheeks were burning red and I was hiding a smile as I faced my essay once again. I was in the library for 2 long hours before I yawned and slammed my laptop shut seeing as I was through with the essay and had emailed it to my professor a good day before the deadline.

It was only 1 pm meaning I had time to run for a quick lunch or even make something at home.

"You're done?" James gazed at me as soon as I stood up. I nodded packing up my stuff "Yep."

"Just chill a bit for me I'm also done." He said and I agreed. We both strolled outside the library still making small chatter with each other.

"So are you sure you don't wanna hang out today?" He asked again. "I mean this new wicked club just opened and I've wanted to check it out for a while now."

I laughed shaking my head "Don't worry dude. Been there, done that already on Friday."

"S'kinda funny when you call me dude." James teased. "Like you're so American."

I rolled my eyes playfully "Right, considering I am from there."

We both cackled like idiots but we didn't seem to care really. Well I didn't until I set my eyes one something that made my eyes nearly bulge out of their sockets.

It was Axel, dressed in form fitting blue jeans, a grey long sleeved shirt with buttons and the sleeves folded to the elbows, a pair of black suede loafers without socks (which looked hella sexy by the way) and black aviators. He was leaning on a car. It took a lot for my jaw not to kiss the ground right then.

"Hello Kendall. It seems like you've forgotten about our meeting today." his voice was smooth and velvet and made me want to bash his head on the hood of that car. And maybe mine too.

"Who's this Kendall?" James asked sounding genuinely confused.

All I could do was stare.

Chapter 5 - A Proper Vagabond

I just want to bring to everyone's attention that this book is rated R so expect some smexy action a lot. If you're fine with that great, but if you have virgin mind I suggest you leave because this is as dirty as they get. But if you don't mind then fine but please no hate. But there isn't any serious smut in this chapter yet but more is coming ;)

Anyways vote+comment+love oreos (ok that's just me). Enjoy!

P.S Please play the song on the side towards the end. You'll see why ;)

"What are you doing here?" I asked surprised and agitated at the same time.

Axel took off his shades and tucking them into his breast pocket. "I told you that I would see you today. And I'm pretty sure that I emphasized today."

My throat felt dry all of a sudden but before I could say anything James spoke up "Who are you?"

"No friend of yours so therefore no business of yours." Axel replied sharply. James glared at him "Don't speak to me like that-"

"I can and I will."

I grabbed James' arm "It's fine. Just let it go." trying to sooth him.

"I thought you didn't have any plans today?" I couldn't miss the accusing tone in his voice but decided to play it off.

"Well not really." I started not really knowing how to explain it "I said we would meet up but kind of forgot about it."

Axel cleared his throat which was a clear indication that he was getting impatient. I fought the urge to roll my eyes at him but gave James a pat instead on the shoulder "So I guess I'll see you later man."

He didn't look too happy "Yeah whatever. Later." I turned to Axel as soon as he was gone "How the hell did you know I was here?"

He shrugged "Lucky guess."

I huffed "Really? Because this seems a lot like stalking to me. And don't tell me you were meeting another friend at the university library because that excuse doesn't cut it. I said that I would see you later today but that doesn't mean you have any right to show up at my place of learning and insult my friend."

Axel sighed "Are you going to get in or not?"

The audacity of this man! Acting like all that came out from my mouth was fresh air not actual meaningful words from a red-blooded human like him. It made me want to the ball my fists and punch that flawless well-trimmed beard of his. Not stroke it, definitely not stroke it.

"Besides if I were stalking you." his voice was a lot lower and he had taken only two strides before being in front of me "I wouldn't ask nicely. I'd throw you over my shoulder and take you on the backseat of my car without a single word." He emphasized on the last three words letting his hot breath deliciously warm up my neck.

This was not fair. No way, evil, dirty and super sexy was not the way to play nicely. At this rate my jeans were already tightening more than naturally allowed and there were several looks we were receiving from curious students.

I cleared my throat "Um let's go."

The bastard was smirking knowing exactly what he had done to me. He opened the passenger door "After you."

I pretended not to act impressed by the state-of-the-art car that we were in. I recognized it as a 2014 Chevrolet Camaro Z/28 from one of the automobile magazines Pierce threw around the apartment. I wasn't a materialistic person but there was no way anyone could not bat an admiring eyelash at this beauty right here.

"Where are we going?" I asked Axel as soon as he got into the car. It took me only a little while to realize that I had just entered the car without thinking or asking about where we were going. Gosh that must be every serial killer's ideal dumb moment.

"Somewhere." Axel replied wearing his aviators. I squirmed internally.

"That's obvious already." I stated not even hiding the sarcasm in my voice. "I'm asking you the name of wherever the hell you're taking me."

He was silent for a while only speaking when the traffic light turned red "I was thinking we could go somewhere for lunch." It obviously wasn't a question, but I could sense that he was silently asking for my approval.

"Ok." I answered quietly. To be honest uncertainty swirled within me but I was excited at the same time. The incident at Red Velvet had left me confused and somewhat scared because I didn't know what he was playing at. I mean he found me on his boat thinking I was some vandalising thug, then only a few hours later he sends me a watch and wants to claim me as his. The situation did make me feel a bit dizzy if you placed yourself in my shoes.

I played with my fingers occasionally stealing glances at Axel. He remained cool and collected behind the wheel, steering left and right with an exaggerated elegance. Of course he would make driving seem like something soulful.

"This is the place." He announced as soon as we stopped in front of a classy looking restaurant. It took me a while to notice that it was actually semi-formal reliving me immensely because I wasn't sure that my current attire of skinny jeans and high tops would be appropriate for a high class restaurant. Even here I still felt out of place somehow.

"I wasn't sure what you liked to eat so I just settled on Italian because obviously everyone likes Italian." He spoke as we entered the restaurant. He shouldn't have made such an assumption because there was no assurance that I liked Italian. But of course everyone likes Italian.

"But what if I didn't like it?" I decided to challenge him.

Axel looked at me for a second "Then I'll just take you somewhere that you'd like." The answer was so obvious that it made me feel stupid for a moment. But Axel placed a hand at the small of my back leading me to our table behind the woman who checked his reservation. Our table was far behind a lot more secluded from the rest which relived me and made me nervous at the same time.

"Your waiter or waitress will be here shortly." She said with a brisk nod before heading off.

"Just for the record I'm still mad at your display in front of the library." I said bluntly once she was out of earshot.

"I'm sorry for that." He sounded sincere.

I nodded looking down at my lap "How did you know where I was? And please the truth this time."

"I actually went to your apartment first but met your roommate instead. He seemed more than pleased to reveal your whereabouts." I made a mental note to thump Pierce properly once I got home.

"Why did you go to my apartment?" I asked.

"Because I wanted to see you. I thought I made that very clear last night." He replied. The waitress arrived, a tall leggy red head with a too cheerful smile. "Hello my name is Sandy and I'll be your waitress for this afternoon." She handed us the menu before retreating.

Axel opened his and glanced briefly before speaking "Did you think about what I asked you?"

"Yes and no." I said nervously.

He hummed dropping his menu on the table "You still seem very hesitant."

"Well you can't really blame me. The same guy who threatened to snap my neck a few days ago suddenly expresses his deep want for me. Could be quite scary if you ask me." I replied slowly.

"I was being cautious back there." Axel stated. The waitress arrived and took our orders before walking quickly.

My heart was beating quickly. I rubbed my hands underneath the table "I really don't understand what you want from me. I mean, you really don't know and I don't know you either. At least not very well. If it's a one night stand or quick bang then I'm not interested."

"If I wanted a one night stand I wouldn't have sent you a thousand pound watch or gone to meet you at your apartment." He said brusquely. "Believe me I never have to chase a conquest hard."

Rubbing his Casanova status in my face, very convincing.

"Then why are you chasing me?" I asked trying not to sound annoyed.

Axel drummed his fingers on the table "Don't think of it as chasing. I'm trying earnestly to convince you into something which would benefit us both and you know it."

The mindless sex would benefit us obviously. But I'm not going to be a chew toy he can play with and toss when he discovers a new toy.

"I'm sure there are a lot of other people who might want you. I'm just in university and a lot younger than you obviously. There should be a lot more people more interesting than me and in your......rank." I said eyeing the table cloth.

"Attraction has no boundaries Kendall." The tingling in my spine. "I'm sure you're aware of that. I want you. Simple as that." He said as if it were really that short and simple. I wanted to say something else but the waitress came with our orders so I decided to shut it for now.

The food was delicious I had to admit. I ordered a lot more than I would usually eat but my breakfast was light and I wasn't paying so why not? Though I managed to eat as delicately as I could because let's face it I was a bit shy of eating in front of Axel. He managed to make a simple activity such as eating so awe-inspiring.

"So." I sipped my lemonade "How old are you exactly?"

Axel stopped for a moment as if he were mildly surprised that I asked that "Ten years on you." I did a quick calculation. He was 29, hmm he clearly wasn't old. We both asked each other some more questions. I learnt that he was born in Oxford but moved to London at a very young age. He studied at University of London, like me, but refused to say exactly what he majored in. A lot of my questions were brushed off or diverted but I didn't press much into it.

"You obviously don't work at Burger King, so where do you work?" I asked.

He chuckled at my sass "Is this an interview?"

"Well we obviously need to know things about each other if we're going to be relating more frequently." I bit my tongue at relating because I wanted to replace it with something else.

He nodded "I don't want to expose all the details at once, but it's legitimate so don't worry." He wanted to remain secretive. That was fine for now anyway.

"And very profiting too." I said dryly rolling my fork in my pasta.

He smirked "Obviously. So where in America are you from?"

"California." I answered without thinking.

"Ah the sunshine state." Axel observed. "Must have been nice growing up with so much sun."

I didn't reply to that so I stuffed a forkful of pasta to avoid doing so. We were silent for a while only focusing solely on our food. But there was still something bugging me.

"Would I need a contract?" I asked.

"Excuse me?"

"I asked if I would a contract or MOU of some sort." I repeated. Axel curled his lip "We're not going to be in some sort of Dom/Sub relationship if that's what you're thinking." I could have sworn that I was the male replica of Anastasia Steele a while ago.

"Then what sort of relationship would it be?"

He leaned in closer so that it was possible to lower his voice "Kendall you're a smart boy. You're obviously attracted to me and I am to you. Let me make this clear; I don't do very well with polyandry and I don't like to share what's mine. If we both agree to this I'm not going to be your Dom and I don't expect you to submit to me. What I expect is for you to recognize my ownership over you because I really don't to share what's mine."

"And you would only be with me." I muttered.

Axel moved back "Yes. Only you."

The promise sounded very enticing at the moment. If I was honest his proposal was sort of benefiting to me. My attraction to him was obvious yes, but apart from physical attraction his personality and some bits of his background were still a mystery to me. I didn't want to get with him only to discover that he was some sort of abuser or secret sadist.

I did have a good gut feeling about him but the missing bits were what worried me.

"Don't overthink it." He brought me from my thoughts carefully sliding his hand onto mine on the table. I tried not to let it show how much that simple action affected me. "If want to say yes do but if you don't want this you're free to walk out that door and I will never bother you again. But for both our sake's I hope you say yes."

I bit my lip; a chance to get out, to run from this without looking back. To be safe. But I would never really be safe with my thoughts and experiences always facing me. Maybe this was what I needed. The thrill of the unknown, something I was unfamiliar with but wanted to embrace instead of fear it. Isn't that why I came down here in the first place?

I had always done things accordingly, followed rules, been nice to everyone, tolerated my stuck up relatives, endured harsh homophobic comments, and patted my roommates back every time he had to puke due to an all-night rave. It was time I took a risk for myself, do something people would think I'd never do.

"I'm not running." I whispered gripping Axel's hand tighter.

He smiled brushing my knuckles with his thumb "Then let's get the hell out of here."

I had never been so fucking turned on in my life.

*****

"You didn't wear your watch." Axel said absently once he parked in front of my complex.

"What?" I asked.

He turned to me calmly placing his hand to cup my cheek "I asked you to wear your watch today and you didn't."

I deliberately didn't wear it but with a good reason. It would be unusual for me to walk around campus with a watch of such magnitude without attracting attention to myself. Anyone would assume that I stole it or some overzealous individual could beat me up and steal it from me.

"It's too flashy." I said lamely.

His hand dipped lower to my waist causing me to shiver visibly "Wear it tomorrow."

"Why?" I asked confused.

Axel smirked pulling me towards without warning "Because I'm taking you to an event." Right now I was straddling him with my back pressed against the steering. I didn't want to attract any attention from my neighbours with the expensive parked in the complex. His hands were freely roaming around my waist, thighs etc. getting my friend below a little excited.

"Formal?" my tone was uneasy.

"Yes but I have it covered." I wanted to ask exactly what he meant by that but was distracted the sinful lips attached to my neck. "I've thought about getting you off."

Me too.

He trailed from the back of my ear down to my collarbone where his previous mark had faded "You smell so good." He murmured sucking on my collarbone intensely making me bite my lip to stop an embarrassing moan from escaping. I was trying desperately not to hit the car horn by mistake. I rubbed myself on Axel creating that delicious friction before he also unconsciously started doing same.

My eyes were shut tight as I focused on how his beard left a slight burn in every inch it skin it came in contact with. He gripped the life out of my ass, bucking his hips to meet my desperate thrusts.

"You like? Do you like it when I touch you like that?" he murmured into my ear.

"Fuck yes."

I was close, so close to letting go and reaching that mind blowing high. "Fuck Axel."

"Oh yeah come like that." And I did clutching his shirt and whimpering because I didn't want to make noise. Axel swore holding my ass tight so I assumed that he also reached a satisfying release.

I slowly came down from my high and tried to move back to the passenger seat but he held me in place though I was starting to feel uncomfortable with jizz in my pants. He mouthed at the dark red hickey on my collarbone "Don't forget the watch."

I tried to fight a smile "I won't."

"Good."

I hopped out of the car but not before Axel kissed me hard with tongue and all almost causing little Kenny to make a reappearance.

"Goodnight Kendall." He said clutching the wheel of his Camaro.

I smirked "Night Axel." before he drove off and I stood there still breathing heavily from the naughty activity I took part in a few minutes ago and wondering what the hell got into me. I'm not that type of guy who goes for a rump in the car. However it made me feel rebellious and cheeky in a good way.

Ignoring the wet patch on my jeans I walked up to my apartment calmly too meet Pierce shirtless on the couch watching How To Get Away With Murder and devouring a huge tub of Ben & Jerry's. his eyes widened when he saw my slightly dishevelled appearance.

"Shit what happened to you mate?" he stood up to get a better look at me.

"Nothing." I replied calmly walking past him.

"Is that a hickey?"

"Maybe." I removed my shoes.

"Did you jizz your pants?"

"Most likely." My socks were next.

His eyes were the size of saucers "Where were you all day?"

"Library." I carried my stuff to my room slamming the door. Only to emerge a few seconds later throwing a shoe at Pierce. "What was that for?" he glared at me.

"Telling a random stranger my location. But thanks anyway."

Chapter 6 - A New World

Warning Mild Sexual Content. Be warned ;)

"Hello? Kendall is that you sweetheart?"

I bit my lip "Yes mom it is."

"Oh sweetie I've missed you so much. You don't call home anymore." I glanced at the clock in my room. It was sometime between 1 and 2 AM but it was the only time I could catch her awake due to the different time zones. The truth was that I couldn't sleep ever since I placed my head on the pillow a few hours ago. It was hot and I felt sweaty and restless until I decided that I had enough credit on my phone to make an international call to my mom.

"Sorry just been busy with college and stuff." I bit my lip because that was only half-truth. I'd had plenty opportunities to call her last week alone despite my schedule.

"Is everything alright sweetie?" her voice was worried. She sounded warm and safe and comforting and home, everything I wanted but couldn't have at the moment.

I swallowed painfully "Yes mom. Just really wanted to say that I miss you."

"Aww sweetie I miss you too. This big house is boring without you or your sister." I held back the bile in my throat "And it's really tiring making dinner for only one except when Paul's around." Paul was the man my mother had been seeing for the past two years and I couldn't really say anything about him except that he was nice and treated my mom like a princess. And he didn't ever try to impose himself as my dad and I was happy he respected that about me.

"I'll probably see you during spring break." I said.

She hummed "Well thank you for calling me out of the blue like this. I really appreciate this."

"Me too mom." And I was sincere.

"Did Mara call you any time this week?" my heart stopped for a moment.

"No."

"Oh." She sounded disappointed "You two should call each other more often."

"It's fine mom." I said hurriedly in a plot to stop the subject from going further. Mom was quiet "I hope you're taking care of yourself like you promised."

"I am."

"Ok. I love you my precious boy."

The tears clogged at my throat almost made it impossible for me to say a single word. "Love you too mom."

The line went dead.

*****

In between all the tossing and crying and thinking and muffling my screams through my pillow and being generally miserable I managed to get some sleep. Only it was too short before I woke up to Pierce staring at me and clutching my comforter.

I grunted covering my head with the duvet until my brain finally registered what I had seen.

"What the hell Pierce!"

He gave a sheepish smile "It's almost noon. You never sleep past nine, even on weekends. I was worried."

At that moment any trace of annoyance was flushed out of my system and I sighed at his thoughtfulness. "Thanks for caring P."

He smiled brightly for a moment "And I also want to know why you came back last night with map-sized hickeys and tried to assassinate me with a shoe on top of it." I really wanted to laugh at his expression but managed to keep a straight face.

"That would be the part where I remind you that it's none of your business." I said sweetly.

Pierce raised an eyebrow "Fine then." He stood up from my bed stretching and I noticed that he was wearing a pair of black sweats and a grey University of Boston t-shirt I'd sworn I lost a while ago. "I guess I'll just eat all those maple and cinnamon spiced pancakes I made by myself."

It didn't take before I dished out the gist to Pierce while stuffing his delicious pancakes in my mouth.

"Wow that guy from the boat?! I knew it was a good idea." He mused while drinking his orange juice. I tried to openly glare at him. And here I was thinking that he'd feel guilty knowing my body might have been fish food.

"So you guys hooked up at the club?" he asked stabbing a strip of bacon.

I shook my head "No but that was when he um.....made the proposal to me."

"And you agreed?"

I nodded slowly. He dropped his fork "So you agreed to like be each other's bang buddies? I'd say friends with benefits but you weren't actually friends in the first place, but you both agreed not to be with anyone else while you're together thereby turning this into some sort of complicated but still vanilla style relationship?"

I thought hard about it before answering. "Yes."

Pierce chuckled "Can't you see this mate? It's like he's Christian fucking Grey and you're all Anastasia Steele expect with short hair and a bigger ass and I'd actually bang you"-

"Whoa this is purely vanilla not all that Dom/Sub nonsense." I explained sternly. "He's not into that anyway."

"And you know because?"

"He told me." I said in a duh tone.

"And you believe him because?"

"Stop it Pierce." I said chewing "Look we both agreed on a simple, non-complicated relationship. We satisfy each other's need and stay with only each other. Simple as that."

"That's what I don't get." Pierce confessed.

"What?" I asked in confusion.

"Kendall you can barely kiss a guy first without knowing his social security number first. Just four days and you're already dry humping this guy in his car." Of course he found out. "And from what you've told me the only time you've slept with someone was in your last two relationships back in America. We've been living together for almost 2 years and it was only last year you were comfortable with me coming into your room."

"What's your point?" I asked him twisting a piece of bacon on my fork.

"You hardly let people in. You'd never kiss someone you don't even know let alone have a meaningless one night stand. For some reason the people around you have to reach a certain level of trust in your mind before they can get halfway. But this guy just bursts into your life in the oddest way ever and suddenly you've agreed to something as serious this."

My throat felt dry. Pierce was right; I wasn't someone who had a lot of friends or relationships or let people around me really. So why had I opened the door for Axel so easily?

"I-I don't really know." I said honestly "Around him it just feels like there's nothing else to hide. I still don't know what I'm doing but it honestly doesn't feel as wrong or weird as it should."

Pierce smiled at me as if he knew something I didn't. "Don't poke at your brain Kenny bear. All I just want is for you to be careful with this."

I nodded "Wait, how did you know we went frisky at the back of his car?"

He gave me a cheeky smile "You just told me."

I spent the rest of the morning chasing him around the flat.

******

"You're so lucky. You get to go to some fancy event in Chelsea while I'm stuck here eating junk food and wanking over Tyler Hoechlin's face." Pierce whined as we spent the whole day going through my closet for what to wear tonight.

I rolled my eyes "He never said it was in Chelsea."

He snorted rolling on my bed "Yeah 'cause a guy with a car like that goes to events in Brent Cross."

I dropped my last article of clothing on the floor. "I have nothing to wear. Maybe I should call and act sick-"

"No!" Pierce shouted. "You are going with that piece of hot ass if I have to steal clothes."

"Yes Pierce please do build up your criminal resume on my account." I said dryly sitting on the edge of the bed. "I don't have anything to wear and it's not like clothes will appear on our doorstep."

The doorbell rang. Of fucking course.

He stood up excitedly running to the door and I trailed behind wondering when my life turned into a cliché fairy-tale.

Sure enough a postman stood outside the door with a box big enough for clothes "Package for Kendall Ross please."

I signed and had to keep Pierce from ripping it open like a kid. When I did open it there was a fancy writing that said Burberry on top.

"It's Burberry! Oh my god this is like too good to be true!" He was all but humping me now. I had to say that I was a bit excited that he sent me clothes as if he had known beforehand that I might have some difficulty in that department.

I carefully opened the box to reveal a light blue blazer with gold buttons. Slim fitted and definitely my size along with black skinny jeans and suede loafers, all of which could be matched with a black V-neck. I wasn't surprised because a guy like Axel had an impeccable sense of style. What he had picked made me feel slightly formal but not in the suit-and-tie way. God knows I hate those so much.

At the bottom of the box was a note as usual.

Don't forget the watch this time

"I would totally fuck you in this outfit." Pierce commented as I checked myself out in the mirror.

"God I hope I won't get raped before I get to the front door." I deadpanned. I had to admit that I looked nice and felt nice also. It only made me more nervous meeting Axel. It felt long overdue and at the same time too soon to do this. Fuck I was scared.

My phone beeped bringing me out of my thoughts.

It was a message from Axel. I didn't even have time to brood over how the hell he got my number because I sure as hell didn't give it to him before opening my messages.

Come outside.

I guess he was here already. I took a deep breath pushing some strands of hair back in place. But not before I grabbed the intimidating Rolex and carefully clasped it on my wrist. It felt heavy and foreign but surprisingly good at the same.

"See you later P." I called out to Pierce as I strode to the front door. He glanced at me from the TV "Don't let anyone fondle your ass too much. It's mine remember."

All this time and I haven't reported him for sexual harassment. Really I don't know why I haven't yet. Probably still keeping him around for his great cooking. I spotted a black town car with a familiar broody looking guy standing beside it. He opened the door and ushered me in silently with the same stoic soulless look on his face.

Oh, it was Mr. Meat- Timothy from the yacht. No wonder he looked at me like his dying wish was to rip my throat with his teeth.

"Hi." Axel said softly alerting me of his presence. "You look gorgeous." He was one to talk. The man looked as though he was sculpted by the gods and sent to torment the rest of us ordinary mortals. He was wearing a tux, the suit well-tailored and probably cost more than my apartments rent. His hair was slicked back with some gel and made me want to pull at it very roughly if you know what I mean. Honestly it took a moment to recover before I could actually say anything

"Thanks. You picked it out so you would know." My throat felt dry and parched like I hadn't had any liquid in the past 24 hours. "And you look amazing yourself."

He nodded brushing my wrist with his fingers "I'm glad you're coming with me tonight." So was I.

"You didn't tell me exactly where we were going." I said.

Axel played with my fingers a little while longer "An art show a friend of mine is hosting." That didn't sound too boring. I was minoring in art myself so maybe this would give me a few pointers. I crossed my legs "I don't think your bodyguard likes me."

"Who? Timothy?" He asked amused. "He doesn't like anyone who's not Kate Winslet."

"Probably why you hired him." I said absently staring outside the window. I could feel Axel's hand creeping up my thigh but I ignored it partially to avoid an increase in my heartbeat. His hand continued till it reached my zipper.

"I love these jeans on you." he said. I noticed that the partition had been set up so that Timothy didn't get a glimpse of us which was probably why he was talking so freely. "They leave nothing to the imagination."

To prove a point he pinched my butt earning a small gasp from me. I tilted my body closer to him and I was almost on his lap. He latched his lips onto my neck sucking it mercilessly until I'm sure it was an unnatural colour. I moaned gripping at his suit cautiously because I didn't want to ruin it before the show.

I was getting hard fast and the tightness of my jeans made me feel uncomfortable.

"You're hard already. Fuck you're so hard right now." He whispered biting down on my ear. I whimpered desperate trying to buck my hips up to his but his grip on my hip was preventing so.

"Don't want you to walk around for half about 2 hours with jizz in your pants." Axel explained. I was frustrated wondering what the hell I would do to make this hard on go down. He dragged my zip down palming me through my boxers causing a groan to erupt from my lips. I bucked my hips into his palm.

"Fuck Axel." I moaned biting my bottom lip. He continued kissing my neck while trying to get me off "You like that babe? Want me to make you come this way?"

"Yes." My voice sounded pained mainly because it was a burden to try and talk with this much pleasure.

He yanked down my boxers taking me complete bare which earned another loud guttural moan.

At a point I was worried that Timothy could hear and that I was going to stain the car seat.

He flicked his wrist "Just like that babe. Let it out just like that." Due to the fact that it had been a while since I had any sexual contact I spurted immediately out on the floor of the town car, little white spurts of come staining Axel's wrist. I was breathing heavily as he provided some tissues and wiped the leather seats. I cleaned myself up with the tissues and wiggled back into my boxers and jeans recovering from the mind blowing orgasm I had just experienced.

"Sorry about that." I apologized to Axel as he tossed away the used tissues trying to ignore how red my cheeks felt.

"It's fine." He brushed off.

Suddenly I felt bad that he had gotten me off and he was left unattended. It was only fair that I returned the favour.

"Do you want me to......?" I glanced down at his pants already moving my hands but he stopped me.

"No, it's fine." He breathed out and I nodded wondering what the hell I had gotten myself into.

Sorry if this chapter is a bit boring. I've been feeling a bit down lately but nothing serious. What do you guys think of Kendall? He's a got a lot more going on than we might think. And on a scale of 1-10, how inappropriate is Pierce? xD

Anyway vote+comment and blah blah blah

Chapter 7 - Always Respect The Artist

I just want to acknowledge that this story now has over 1K reads and although it doesnt seem like much I'm happy because of how much the numbers have grown withing these short few days.

Anywaysssssssss. I just want to point out one more time that this book is rated R for a reason. If you can't handle it please refrain from reading the content. I'm only going to say this once thanks and enjoy xx

After our very steamy moment Axel and I didn't talk much again. Mostly because he kept on taking calls and I busied myself with texting Pierce and answering all of his inappropriate questions. It turned it was at some fancy gallery in Chelsea but I didn't let him know that. He had to remain in the dark or else I would be taunted continually.

"We're here." Axel announced as soon as the car stopped. "Please park around the back Timothy." He added before getting out of the car. I got out on my own side immediately pushing my jacket closer because it was a bit chilly. Early evening already.

"Let's go." He placed his hand on the small of my back guiding me into gallery as I also tried to pretend the sudden action didn't affect me. Inside was cool and white, instantly emitting a sophisticated artsy glow even though we were just in the corridor and the paintings weren't in sight yet.

There were several men and women chatting together all dressed impeccably as only the London high society could. A lot of them approached Axel with airy greetings and talked about common things of interest for a while. I was pointedly ignored but it didn't bother me at all; it's not like I had anything to say to these people. At least he kept his hand on my back not making me feel like a complete outsider which was thoughtful enough for me.

To be honest I felt out of place and with good reason. It wasn't my fault that I didn't know anything about the weather in France or who was dominating the stock market. Ok maybe that was a little presumptuous but you catch my drift.

But when we did enter the main room I was in awe. The paintings I saw were good, outstanding to say the least. Most of them were a bit different, a lot bolder, but somehow you could sense the meaning in them. Even from afar. I was expecting something different, perhaps a bunch of happy-go 'broken hearted/my mother's dying' mediocre paintings that nobody really understood but were glad to spend huge amounts of money on it because it proved something.

No this was different. And different was good.

"Who's the artist?" I asked Axel after sometime when we were finally free of corporate wolves.

"A friend of mine. His boyfriend happens to be my best mate from childhood and so it was a must for me to attend." He replied signalling a waiter with a tray full of champagne.

"Are you sure you're legal enough to drink?" he teased handing me a glass.

"Hardy har." I replied dryly. It was my first glass of champagne but I wasn't going to let it be known. It had a chalky, flinty taste which made me wonder what all the fuss was about but it was genuine Moet so I sucked up anyway.

I took another sip "May I go check out some other paintings?" it made me feel kind of stupid to ask for permission but Axel had invited me in the first place and it only seemed fair in case he just wanted me by his side all night.

"Of course." He dismissed as I eyed another gentleman approaching his for what be another long greeting.

I strolled around a little ignoring the hordes of men and women talking in loud voices gazing at the paintings and making my quiet analysis on them. In fact I saw some which would definitely make a great addition to the piece I was writing for my Fine Art professor. My phone was buzzing annoyingly in my pocket so I switched it off.

There was a piece in particular that caught my eye.

It was of a little girl holding a rose, her clothes tattered and her appearance ripped in the most tragic way ever. But she was smiling. Goddammit she was smiling. So brightly, like there was nothing wrong, like it was a simple scrap or bruise. It struck me so deeply in the chest. It's not like I understood it completely but it made every cell in my body come alive in complete awe.

"It's my favourite painting too." I heard a voice behind me.

I turned to see a man-no boy, probably only a few years older me if we weren't the same age. His face was lit up, like a torch with unquenchable fire. He had messy blonde hair pushed back and an American eagle scarf tied over his head. He was wearing a blue long sleeve folded at the elbow and ripped jeans. The only thing that seemed appropriate enough for the occasion were his brown dress shoes. I wondered how he wasn't thrown out already. He definitely stood out amongst everyone.

"Huh?"

He moved closer to my side "It's my favourite in this collection I mean."

"Oh." I looked back at the painting admiring it. "It's striking. Forces you to stare and want to know more even if you can't understand."

"American accent, cool." His face lit up with another smile and it made me wonder of this guy could ever frown in his life. "That's one way to put it." The guy was cute, twinky was another term I was have used if I didn't find it so awfully degrading. His frame was thin and smallish but at the same time lanky and long.

"I hate suits." He said subtly letting me know he knew I was checking out his attire. "They make me feel like I'm in some cardboard prison."

"Me too." I replied raking my eyes over the painting once again.

"Rebecca." I read out loud at the bottom. I glanced back at it "It's really wonderful. If I had a single cent to my name I'd probably pester the artist into selling it to me. I mean I'm that desperate."

He laughed and it was rich and full of life almost making me envious. "That's a first. I'm pretty sure you'd be the only one who'd truly appreciate it unlike the rest of these knobs bumping into each other like it's Pac man."

I chuckled at that "What about you? Get forced to accompany the 'rents?"

He shrugged "Not really. It's not like I can skip out on my own art exhibit."

I nearly choked on my champagne. He was the artist?! Urgh suddenly I had this horrible feeling for judging him so early for his eccentric clothing even though I was already warming up to him a little.

He smiled sheepishly "Sorry. I'm not really one to announce my presence in a room."

I coughed "That's fine. I'm just glad I critiqued your work rightly. Anyways I'm Kendall and still sadly in Uni so I'm not yet at your level."

He grinned exposed his charming white teeth "Martin Doyle. I'd like to call myself an artist but I think I'm a bit too organized for that." We both shared a small laugh. I guess this was the boyfriend of Axel's best friend. He seemed pretty young, quite an accomplishment to have your artwork displayed for such high bidders.

"I'm not that young." Martin said as if he read my mind. "Just turned 21 last month though my boyfriend still likes to call me short cake." It wasn't with cocky or exaggerated gusto he said it. More like someone who shares that they stubbed their toe once. Just simplicity. Like he didn't even care if I might have been homophobic or not.

"Still young though. Congrats anyway." I said dropping my now empty glass on a passing tray. "It's hard really to get people to view your work."

He snorted "If it were up to me they would all be locked up in a room in my apartment where no one could see it except me. Unfortunately my boyfriend thinks that art is only appreciated when cocky pricks line up to drool on it and pay large amounts enough to get a whole family through university."

I smiled "But you can't be complaining about the last part. Your boyfriend sounds like a very wise guy."

Martin gave me a thoughtful look "I suppose since I'm the cute one he should get something." This guy was something else. If only I could keep him as a long lost twin.

"Here's the man of the hour." I heard Axel's voice from behind sending tingles through my body. Axel appeared with another equally attractive man with brunette hair and an Armani suit beside him. "Well done Martin."

"Axel!" he gave him a cheerful hug before pecking the man beside him "Hi babe."

Axel placed his hand on my shoulder "This is my date Kendall. Kendall please meet Spencer and Martin. The award winning Andy Warhol and his knob of a boyfriend."

Spencer grinned "Takes one to know one mate. And nice to meet you Kendall."

"You too." I replied politely.

"We've been talking but he wasn't nice enough to tell me that he was your date." Martin said but with no actual heat behind his words. I smiled "Sorry about that."

"It's fine sweetheart." He assured before turning to his boyfriend "I hope you've been behaving yourself. Remember our deal no more than half a glass of champagne."

Spencer laughed kissing his forehead "Relax babe I haven't even had one. Been surviving on the diet Pepsi I nicked at the back." Spencer was obviously older than him but still managed to act like a schoolchild being scolded when it came to Martin.

Martin seemed satisfied with his answer and planted a chaste kiss on his lips "We'd better socialise a bit and get it over with. Nice meeting you Kendall."

"Same." I replied with a smile watching him drag Spencer across the room. I was alone with Axel and it got me wishing I had another glass of champagne.

His hand dipped lower on my back "Are you enjoying yourself?"

I nodded "You didn't tell me you had such a prodigy as a friend."

He chuckled "Martin is definitely talented. Tends to get a bit carried away but luckily Spencer grounds him."

"They balance each other." I murmured watching the two interact from the other side of the room. I turned back to Axel "Thank you for bringing me."

"You're welcome." He answered smoothly. I gulped "You never actually told me what you do for a living."

His face fell for a moment, like he wasn't expecting me to ask that but regained his composure quickly "Ah yes that."

"It's fine if you don't want to talk about it." I offered.

He shook his head "No it's fine. I just don't like talking about it too often. I work at Fletcher Shipping company, well more like own half of it." I wasn't familiar with the name but it sounded like one of those well-known companies you heard on the news.

Stinking rich. Hmm, what else is new?

"At least it's not illegal." I joked. He gave a flicker of a smile "Boring is what it is." Wonder what he meant by that.

Axel gave at me for a while "You looking stunning you know."

"Thank you.....again." now was the time I really needed more champagne to cover my face with so that he wouldn't notice my red cheeks. Oh no, not now. We were in an art gallery filled with people this was not the right time for my body to rebel.

I felt his hand snake around my waist pulling me back "I've been hoping to get alone with you for some time tonight." He murmured to my ear.

I cocked my head to the side "But you've been alone with me. Is there anything in particular you want?" I asked hiding my smirk.

He smirked "You like the chase huh?"

"I don't know what you're talking about." I feigned innocence but he wasn't buying it. My body was pressed against his and I had to look around quickly in hopes that we weren't attracting any attention. "We're in public."

Axel raised an eyebrow "Your point?"

So he wanted to play like that? I bit my bottom lip "If you're into that kind of thing then." I shrugged brushing my thigh over his zipper. He stiffened making me smile on the inside "What are you doing?"

"Nothing." I answered as if he asked if I was part Martian.

His hold on my waist tightened "God you're so delectable. I could take you right now, right here."

"So you are into that kind of thing." I said in half jest and half breathlessly. Axel hovered his lips dangerously over mine "What if I am?"

Holy shit! What was he implying? I hoped that Pierce wasn't right and he secretly wanted a Dom/Sub relationship. But he made it crystal clear from the beginning that he wasn't interested in such. His need for possession wasn't extended to submission.

"What do you want Axel?" I asked putting only an inch of space between us.

"Go down to the corridor we first came in through. Take a left and go into the men's loo. Wait for me there." I bit my lip feeling my pants tighten at all the prospects those words held but myself before I got ridiculously hard in front of all these people.

"Ok." I whispered before slipping from his grasp.

I kept my cool walking past until I got to the corridor. I followed Axel's directions and found myself in the men's bathroom. I looked below all the stalls and luckily no one else was there. I took a deep breath leaning by one of the sinks.

The door opening startled but I noticed that it was Axel. He locked the door and grabbed me roughly, kissing me long and dirty. The kiss surprised me a little, I mean he didn't strike me as someone who enjoyed kissing apart from hickey's and stuff. I just never noticed him leaning towards me or any of that.

"You little minx, you enjoy teasing me don't you?" he groaned pressing his front on mine. I threw my head back replying breathlessly "Do you want me to lie?"

Axel grabbed my ass and squeezed the very life out of it while kissing my throat "So fucking perfect." He murmured. I moaned at the friction our crotches rubbed together created. I fiddled with his zipper while desperately still kissing him until I got it down.

"Wanna blow you." I managed to get out.

Axel didn't reply; instead he just leaned over at the sink giving me the leverage to do so. I got on my knees pulling down his pants and boxer letting his dick free. It was an impressive length making me wonder how the hell all of it would fit into my mouth but I could chicken out yet. I tested the waters placing my mouth over the tip and let go with a pop earning a hiss.

"Don't you fucking dare." He threatened.

I smiled cheekily before taking the entire thing in my mouth causing Axel to groan and swear at the same time. He bucked his hips forward forcing himself further into my mouth. Thank goodness I had no gag reflex. Axel ran his hands through my hair "You're so good at this Kenny. I love fucking your mouth."

I flicked my tongue over his tip as answer to that making him push my head closer. Saliva was dripping down my chin as I anxiously bobbed my head over Axel's length enjoying all the sounds and cuss words that flew from his mouth. I blew for about 20 seconds more before he told me to stop. I looked at him confused because he hadn't even cum yet.

"I want to finish inside you." he said finally pulling my chin off him. I stood up yanking my jeans down to my ankles along with my boxers. Axel turned me so I was leaning forward on the sink massaged my ass "Have I ever told you that you have an amazing arse?"

"No."

He bit into my neck "Well you have an amazing ass."

"I want you inside me now." I tried to keep from whining. I felt something wet and cool at my entrance that I figured to be lube that Axel probably kept in his pocket or something. He fingered my hold making me grip the edge of the sink and moan shamelessly. I really hoped that there was no one in the stalls or this would be tragic.

"Axel." I whined.

"Shhhh babe, want you to be loose for me yeah?" he kissed my neck all the way to the back of my ear. I could barely say ok, I just kept bucking my hips back to reach his touch. I heard plastic tear, which I guessed was a condom.

"Is it your first time?" he asked me probably giving me a chance to back off.

I shook my head "It's just been a while is all."

"Good."

I felt his tip invade my hole and I held the sink so tight that my knuckles turned white. The stretch and burn felt good and hurt at the same time. He was only halfway in which meant that I would have to wait a bit before any action could happen.

"You ok?" he asked sounding concerned.

I clenched my teeth "I'm fucking fine." I guess he took this as a go ahead to go completely inside earning a harsh gasp.

"So tight." Axel commented placing his head on my back. "Can I move please?"

I took two deep breaths "Yeah."

He took a careful thrust and I thought I would burst. It felt delicious and raw and I wanted him all the way now "Oh jeez fuck me."

Axel took another thrust inside but this was harder than the last. He started thrusting faster into me making me buck my hips to meet his touch. He hit my prostrate and every bundle of nerves in me went instantly electrocuted and I let out a howl.

"Fuck Axel! Shit fuck yeah!"

His thrust got faster and my knees went weaker hardly holding my body anymore.

"So good, taking all of me in. So good for me Kenny." He groaned clawing my hips and leaving very visible marks on them. "Mine, shit you're mine."

"Yours." I whimpered feeling that familiar boiling at the pit of my stomach.

"Not yet." He pulled out of me and made me face him before pushing me to sit on the counter. He thrust into me making me scream out because that was a sensitive angle.

"Oh fuck fuck fuck fuck!" I cried out as he placed my leg over his shoulder. His grip bruised my thighs but I didn't care. All my mind was focused on was hitting my prostrate over and over. Axel swore "Look at you. God I'm going to fuck you so good."

"Yes." I could barely even say.

We went like that for a while until he finally hit it and I came hard all over my stomach without warning. Good thing I pulled my shirt up before then.

Axel took two more thrusts before joining me in my high and cumming inside his condom. I breathed out "Well fucking hell." That was more intense than any sexual experience I'd ever had before and I was in two previous relationships. He pulled out and tied the condom before throwing it into the trash. He also helped me with some tissues I used to clean up before pulling my boxers and jean up.

"We need to get you checked. I hate using those." He spoke referring to the condoms in the bin.

"We should probably get going now." I suggested. "Before an angry mob breaks the bathroom door or something."

"Good idea." Axel answered looking slightly amused.

We managed to subtly make our way out of the bathroom one after the other but thankful no had wanted to use the men's room all the time we were inside. Hopefully the smell of sex wasn't too strong.

Just before we could make it out of the entrance I heard someone call out to us. I turned to see Martin coming towards us. "Going already?"

"Sadly yes. I have an early meeting and Kendall has some lectures too." Axel said smoothly as if he hadn't been engaging in any naughty activities a few minutes prior.

"Oh." He looked almost disappointed but recovered quickly. "I just wanted to say I tried to keep that painting for you but it was the first one bought surprisingly."

"Really?" I was surprised but somehow angst at the same time. It's not like I could afford it but I really did like the painting. "Thanks but you can't keep a painting for me that would be a lot really."

He scoffed "It's better off with you than all of those unappreciative spoilt knobs."

I laughed "Well thanks I guess."

Axel cleared his throat "We really have to get going now."

"Right." Martin gave him a friendly hug "Thanks for coming and bring your amazing American date."

"You're welcome." Axel replied with an equally friendly smile of his own. He hugged me also "Hope I see you soon."

"Me too. Bye." I waved at him. Timothy had brought the town car around so I quickly hurried in since it was cold. Once we were in the car neither of us said anything for the entire ride. In my case I really had nothing to say and no way to build up a topic. I didn't know what was going on in Axel's mind so I definitely didn't know his reason.

When we got to my apartment he surprised me by pulling me in for a kiss. This one was soft and chaste, nothing like any of our other kisses.

"I'll call you ok?" he said softly.

I nodded "Goodnight."

And I was walked up to my apartment I couldn't ignore the fluttery feeling blocking my chest and terrifying me at the same time.

Pic of Martin to the side. Isn't he a cutie?

Chapter 8 - Friends And Foes Of The Heart

Sorry this so short. Been up to a lot lately

Currently I was sitting in my Literature class taking notes as the professor tried to get us through the emotional complexities of War and Peace. Or at least I was trying to but an unlikely distraction in the form of Clarissa Downer was intent on ruining one of my favourite classes for me. And let me tell you she was getting there.

She seated beside me wearing white shorts and a blue crop top that said Naughty. It seemed to get the attention of a lot of guys and I was desperately wishing that one of them would grab her away from me. In fact I was willing to pay. Why couldn't she be interested in any of the other normal straight guys?

But no, she kept on slamming Post it notes on my MacBook with little messages like "Please go out with me babe." Or "You look so serious it's turning me onnnnnn." And the worst "Your lips look sad, can I rub them with mine and make them better?"

I would rather lose my virginity to The Rock. Twice. Like this isn't third grade, who the fuck still passes notes in college?

Until I had it tattooed on my forehead that I thought vaginas were ugly, maybe she would back off. But knowing Clarissa her half brain would only pick the words vaginas before flinging herself at me thereby doing the opposite of what I hoped to achieve. I was always at a loss when it came to dealing with this girl. Honestly I wouldn't even be sitting next to her if I hadn't come late to lecture and all the seats were filled and the one beside her was conveniently the only one left. I was actually fine with sitting on the floor but surprisingly some people actually find that barbaric. Humph!

Anyways I had only three minutes left before this lecture ended and I intended to run as fast as I could before Clarissa could even breathe.

"And I would like that emailed to me no later than the 26th." Professor Harris repeated again but I shoved it at the back of my mind as I grabbed my stuff into my messenger bag before she could even look up.

"Miss. Downer may I have a word?" the professor asked and it took all that was within me not to kiss his bald head in delight. She scowled but had to talk to him. Probably about all her pending references.

I breathed in a sigh of relief until I spotted James walking down my side.

"James!" I called out.

He turned around confused but eased up when he saw it was me "Oh it's you Kendall."

"Hi James I haven't seen you while." I said casually as he stood in front of me but seemed a little weary.

He scoffed "Well last time I saw you your boyfriend threatened me." He was obviously referring to what went down with Axel at the library.

"He's not really my boyfriend." I tried to explain "We're just.....um seeing each other." Gosh there really was no easy way to explain this. Axel and I were in an intimate relationship but it wasn't as intimate as James thought. "It's not something I can really explain."

"And you told me that you didn't have any plans yet he storms up like I was gonna kidnap you or something." His tone had a tinge of accusation which made me gulp.

"I can explain that one. I kinda forgot he was coming over and everything was really confusing then"-

James shook his head "Mate you don't have to lie to me. I don't care if you're gay; I think I've made that clear a lot of times. Just don't lie to me ok? Tell me whenever you have plans so I don't feel like a fucking idiot."

His tone made me feel guilty but I really didn't know how to explain it to him.

"I'll see you later." I offered.

"Yeah." He replied absently. "I've got a class now anyway." before treading past me like nothing happened.

What was his problem? I mean James had never really made it known that he cared about whoever I hung out with. We never used to see each other outside of Pierce and the rest so why was he so worked up about this? I'll admit I would be confused if something like that happened to me but this was James for Pete's sake. It took him three tries to remember my name when we first met. He doesn't care that much.

So why was he acting like I had betrayed him somehow?

My thoughts were brought to an abrupt halt when I felt my phone buzz in my pocket indicating I had a text. I brought it out and noticed that it was from an unknown number. My heart lurched involuntarily at the thought that it could be a ploy from Mara since I wasn't picking any of her calls.

Hi Kendall it's me Martin. I got your number from Axel if that's ok.

Martin. My lips formed an unconscious smile when I remembered the eccentric artist from the night back. I shot him a quick reply.

No it's fine. What's up?

He replied immediately.

I've just got some free time on my hands. Would you like us to meet up for lunch somewhere? If only you're free.

Literature was my last lecture for the day. Initially my plan was to spend some extra time at the library throughout the afternoon but I had pulled two all-nighters within the past week and decided that maybe it wouldn't be fine to give myself some time off. My G.P.A of 4.0 wasn't going anywhere yet.

I'll pay so don't worry ;)

Sure I'm free. That sealed the deal.

K, meet me at Colby's Crunch. It's not too far from the university I think. I knew where it was. I had dropped by a few times and their sandwiches were to die for.

Okay :)

I took a bus which was just fifteen minutes away from the main campus to the restaurant Martin told me to meet him at. It was pretty easy to find, just across the road from the bus stop. I spotted him right away; instead of a scarf he had on a purple bandanna and a black short-sleeved tee with matching jeans that looked like they were painted on his body. How did a human managed to survive in those.

I love skinny jeans but even I have a limit.

He looked up from his phone and smiled brightly when he saw me "Hey Kendall glad you could make it. I was just feeling lonely this afternoon and didn't want to have lunch alone."

I pulled back a seat and placed my messenger bag beside the table "Me too. Thanks for bringing me out from the nightmare that is Uni life."

He laughed "It's the cons that make you love it more. What are you studying anyway?"

"Oh I'm an English Major." I replied. "And I'm writing some novel that might never get published anyway."

Martin nodded "That's cool. You gonna be the next Leo Tolstoy?"

I grinned "Hardly. Even though Anna Karenina is my favourite book of his."

"I love reading. I've read all manner of books from Oscar Wilde to Chinua Achebe and I'm still pretty sure I've got a lot more. I think I read almost as much as I paint." He said wistfully. That was pretty impressive. I'm a Literature but I haven't gotten around reading as much as I'd like.

"When I was younger I was this close to being a writer, but art will always be my thing." A waiter arrived and took our orders. I ordered a burger and fries with a coke since I wasn't so hungry but Martin had a Caesar salad and chicken wrap with water.

"Hey I forgot to congratulate you last night. How many paintings did you sell?" I tore my ketchup packet open.

Martin gave me a shy smile "Well all of them. In fact I'm heading to Central London tomorrow because I have a few that I need to deliver."

I smiled genuinely "That's great. I mean you really deserve it." He wrinkled his nose a bit "I guess. But I really feel bad that you didn't get that painting."

"It's fine really. I mean it would be kind of weird to give your expensive artwork to some dude you've just met." I tried to reason.

He shook his head "I just feel like you had so much to relate to it more than anyone else." But deep within myself I really adored that painting. It seemed silly and a tad bit weird that he was so anxious to give it to me but secretly I was glad.

"I can't remember the last time I ate proper junk food." He mused opening his water.

"Why is that?" I asked dipping my fry into some ketchup.

He shrugged "Spencer hardly eats them anymore as doctors' orders so I do the same to encourage him and now it's a habit." Wow, that was pretty selfless of him. I mean giving up his eating habits to encourage his boyfriend to eat healthier.

"That's really great. I mean most people couldn't do that for their spouse or partners." I said thoughtfully.

"For me it didn't seem like I had a choice. I'd shave my head if it comes to his well-being." He said without hesitation. It wasn't a boasting or something said to impress it just sounded like genuine truth coming from his mouth. I wondered how it felt to care for someone that way.

"How did you and Axel meet anyway?" he asked curiously. I swallowed my food "It's kind of a funny story."

Martin snorted "It's always a funny story." I told him what happened on the boat and how I was scared and how we made a deal at a club. He listened intently only not making a single sound all the time I talked. When I finished he sipped his water "That's kind of unusual, I mean the relationship you guys have going on."

"It's mostly sex. Nothing unusual about that." I blurted out.

He curled his lip "I've known Axel for a long time, since I was 18. He doesn't do stuff for people like that."

I scrunched my face in confusion "Like what?"

Martin sighed "He's never taken anyone on a date before. Like ever and I'm serious Kendall. He fools around occasionally but he never publicly takes anyone out, let alone buys them expensive stuff. In fact the only people he's ever gotten presents for are me, Spencer and his dad. Maybe you could include the charities he donates to every year. You could just basically brand him as a no commitment, one night only kind of guy. One of the reasons I was eager to meet you the other night." He added with a small smile.

"Oh. So what are you trying to say?" I asked playing with the straw of my drink.

He shrugged "I'm not jumping into conclusions or judging anyone. I'm just saying that it's a different side of him. Maybe it's good."

I nodded absently thinking back to what Pierce said. Maybe we weren't so different after all. It still baffled me, what Martin said about him. I'll admit that Axel was damn hard to, like really hard. He reacted differently than you would expect but never really did fall short of expectations. I mean his physical appearance was one thing, but his personality intrigued me immensely.

My phone rang. It was Mara again. I ignored the prickles at the back of my neck and cancelled the call.

"Someone calling?" he asked curiously.

"Not important." I brushed off. We ate the rest of our lunch in silence until Martin had to go visit the loo. My phone rang again and I was so close to tossing it out the window until I saw that it was Axel calling me.

"Hi." I answered.

"Hello Kendall." His voice was deep and raspy and sent thought into my head that shouldn't be there. "I was just wondering if I could see you. Where are you now?" I had wanted to see Axel the day before but we were both busy so it had to be put off. Now I couldn't help the bubbly anxious feeling at the bottom of my stomach.

"Um I'm actually having lunch with Martin now but after that you could come to my apartment since I'm free for the rest of the day." I curled my lip.

"I'm actually in my office right now and I'm too busy to step out now. Um, just ask Martin to bring you over. I'm pretty sure he could do that." He suggested.

"He just went to the bathroom but I'll ask him when he gets out."

"Good." The line went dead before I could say anything else.

Martin came out wiping his hands on the back of his jeans "Any problem?"

"No Axel called me and wanted me to meet him in his office. I wanted to know if you could take me there?" I bit my bottom lip.

"Sure no problem." He replied enthusiastically "I was gonna drop by Spencer's office anyway unless he's in court."

"Court?"

"He's a lawyer." He explained. Martin paid for the meal before leading me out of the restaurant to his black Audi A8. I know it seemed awfully judgemental of me but it was pretty impressive for a 21 year old to drive an A8. I strapped in trying my best to listen to Martin rave about the new car smell while trying to ignore how loud my heart thumped in my chest as I thought of seeing Axel.

Chapter 9 - Teach Me

This chapter's got some major spoilers so pay attention xx

It only occurred to me moments after being on the road that I had no idea where Axel's office was. It was only when Martin parked that I was in awe of the tall structure that was Fletcher Tower. And to think that Axel owned half of that.

"The company owns that entire building?" I asked him.

"Yeah but they lease it out since they obvious can't use all the space." Martin replied slamming the door closed. He pushed his hair back with his fingers despite the bandanna "Come on." He led me through the marble ground reception which made me feel a bit embarrassed for wearing combat boots since they squeaked on the polished floor.

We took the elevator to the 12th floor where I assumed Fletcher Shipping was situated in. We were greeted by a red-haired receptionist who seemed very familiar with Martin.

"The office is down by the left. I'd like to take you there but I really need to get to Spencer's like now." He explained. I nodded giving him a side hug "Thanks for lunch. It was really nice to see you again."

"You too Ken doll." He gave me that signature sun-rivalling smile of his before strutting off to the elevator. I moved stiffly towards the direction he pointed me to meeting a strawberry haired receptionist with a too tight shirt working furiously on her computer.

"Excuse me." She snapped her head to look at me.

"Yes?" she replied eyeing me as though she wasn't entirely sure how I got into the building.

I swallowed "Um, I'm here to see Axel. He told me to come meet him in his office."

She dropped her pen "Who are you?"

"Kendall Ross."

She narrowed her eyes at me "Look Mr. Gold isn't receiving any visitors right now. He's instructed me not to let anyone disturb him." What the hell was her problem?! I didn't appreciate the way she kept looking at me like I was dirt on the carpet.

"Look I'll call him"-

"That won't be necessary." She cut me off pretty rudely. I opened my mouth about to utter another of protest but Axel came out of his office saving me the trouble. "What's the problem Stacie? I thought I told you I was expecting someone."

"Well earlier today you said that you didn't want to be disturbed." The tight shirt blonde I assumed was called Stacie said without looking at me. What the heck was the bitch saying?!

"But about an hour ago I told you that I was expecting someone and to let them up." Axel said tightly. Stacie shuffled some papers "Sorry sir. I was just following instructions."

"Then use that brain of yours and listen whenever I tell you something. I told you specifically at 5 to let in the young man coming and I don't tolerate you disobeying my orders unless you'd like to take your *CV somewhere else." He said firmly. "Ok?"

She shrivelled back like a child who's been scolded for being naughty in front of other adults. "I'm sorry it won't happen again."

"It better not." He turned to me and placed his hand on my back "Sorry about that. I'll just get my stuff then we can go." I nodded "Ok."

He went back into his office while I left standing there awkwardly with Stacey who was pretending to be absorbed in her work but I could see the steam radiating off her. I didn't know what her problem with me was but she didn't seem too keen on letting her boss have visitors.

Huh.

"Let's go, Timothy's bringing the car around." Axel emerged with a briefcase and placed his hand on the small of my back, catching me off guard again. This was his office so I didn't think he'd be so open with me......that way at least. I definitely didn't want to be the latest topic on the office gossip amongst the employees and that wouldn't look too good for Axel either.

"Sorry about that I have no idea what's wrong with Stacey. One more strike from that girl and I'm going to fire her." He apologized once we were outside.

I clung to my messenger bag "No really its fine. Maybe she was in a bad mood or something."

"Well that's a pretty stupid excuse to flaunt my orders. Her personal peeves shouldn't stop her from working properly." He dropped harshly like cement. "The way she treated you was unacceptable." I couldn't help but feel my cheeks grow a tinge of red. It shouldn't feel this weird having him defend me.

Timothy brought the town car around and opened the door for me with his built-in stoic expression present. At least it didn't feel like he was going to snap my neck into two this time.

"So where are you taking me?" I asked finally settling in the luxurious town car that still made me feel out of place.

"To my place." Axel replied without looking up from his phone. With his tone he might as have added 'duh' at the end. Although I fear that's a strictly American thing, no pun intended. I stole a glance at him since he was very much occupied with his phone.

He looked powerful; his hair moulded backwards perfectly with the expensive gel I sniffed the night at the art exhibit, not a single strand out of place. His suit was grey today, well-tailored and clung to his body admirably. Probably Armani or some other famous brand. Overall he was breath taking and definitely all man.

Maybe a man who confused the hell out of me sometimes but nevertheless he was impossibly to resist.

"See something you like?" he asked rather coyly but it was obvious he knew I had been undressing him with my eyes.

I rolled my eyes "Maybe I'm just looking outside the window."

Axel turned to me "I had no idea that my window was much more interesting than yours." I'm pretty sure I heard Timothy fight a laugh. At least we're getting somewhere. I huffed crossing my arms over my chest "Well if it so what?"

He chuckled "Whatever you say."

When we pulled up at a well maintained apartment complex that my crummy little flat had nothing on.

"Thank you Timothy." He said smoothly.

"Ok sir." Timothy replied driving the car into the garage I was sure.

"Good evening Mr. Gold." The doorman greeted.

"Evening Hansel." Axel replied guiding me to the elevator and pressing the button for the penthouse. Of course I thought to myself.

The elevator door opened and I was almost taken aback by the luxurious apartment. I mean Axel was a man with great taste so I shouldn't really be surprised. Most of the furniture was white, like the long couch and the two comfy cushion chairs by the side. There was a low rise coffee table in the middle with several magazines scattered across.

"Is this your place?"

"No I just come here to kick off my shoes and go home." Right, dumb question.

All in all it was very clean and well organized like he'd hardly spent any time in here at all. There was a cool looking balcony also.

"You have a great place." I commented.

He shrugged his jacket off his shoulders "Like you'd expect less." His tone was smug, but he was right. He tore off his tie dumping it on the couch before unbuttoning his shirt next making me gulp. He did have tattoos like I guessed, several of them. Honestly it surprised me but still made him look sexy as hell with all that glorious ink scattered all over his body.

"You have tattoos."

Axel raised an eyebrow "Evidence of careless youth I'll admit. Well maybe not so careless since the last one I got was a few months ago. Are you ok?"

I blinked "Why?"

"You've been standing there without moving or dropping you bag." He finally removed his belt and let his pants fall down and kicking them off exposing those gloriously toned legs of his.

I removed my messenger bag and placed it neatly on the couch closet to me "So what now?"

"Come here." He said softly but I could hear the hidden order. I eagerly did so my chest thumping excitedly about the moment I'd been dreaming about. Axel groped my sides and kissed me hungrily without giving me any room to breathe or recover. I rubbed myself on his crotch causing him to groan and grab me even harder.

It was rough and I totally wanted it.

Without thinking I yanked my shirt off throwing it to some distant corner of the living room. He caressed my butt "Jump."

I did so wrapping my legs around his waist. He was able to manoeuvre us to what I guessed was his bedroom and dropped me on the bed. I didn't even take time to admire the king-sized bed or any of the other furniture. All I wanted were his lips on mine.

"Take off your jeans."

I obeyed wiggling out of my skinny jeans and tossing them over on the floor before Axel pushed his way in between my legs and attacked my already puffy lips.

"Oh fuck." I moaned when he proceeded to bite my earlobe. He kissed my neck all the want to my collarbone before leaving a very large throbbing mark there. I buried my fingers in his hair pushing him down harder because of how much I needed him. "Shit Axel I want you now." I moaned arching my back off the bed.

Axel didn't answer me. He only kissed me some more before pulling away to search for something in his bedside before emerging with lube and a condom. He threw my boxers off and paused taking the time to study my naked appearance. This was the first time I was seeing the other parts Axel apart from his dick and I had to say that all his lean muscle and sweat slicked tattoos did a number on my hormones.

He brought his finger to my lips "Suck."

I did exactly that sucking his finger and making all the erotic noises I knew that he turned him on. Axel swore at my little act and so I made sure to look at him widening my eyes like an innocent kid. He withdrew his finger stroking my lip with his thumb "What do you want eh?"

"Please fuck me Axel. I need you." I whined wanting nothing more than him being inside me and moving without stopping. My erection was throbbing and leaking pre-come already.

"Shhhh." He placed a finger on my lips while using the bottle of lube to coat my entrance. "Spread your legs for me babe." I spread them eagerly waiting for him to fuck me senseless. His two fingers stretched me open making my back arch from the bed, bucking to the rhythm of his hands.

"Love watching you like this. So responsive, like the little mix you are." He purred and I wanted to cry out from the frustration building up from not having him inside me. Axel finally removed his fingers "Ready for me?"

"Yes." I nearly screamed.

He grinned slowly pushing down his CK boxers, exposing that impressively mouth-watering length of his. He knelt on the bed lining his dick against my hole just to tease me some more.

"Just fuck me Axel!"

Suddenly he shoved himself into me without warning and I was overwhelmed by how full I felt and how big he was. Axel lifted my thighs wrapping them around his waist before taking a slow, full thrust. It felt like the air had been kicked out my lungs.

"Oh f-f-fuck." I stuttered.

"Are you ok?" his eyes flashed with concern for a second at whether he hurt me.

I gritted my teeth "Move. Please." He didn't waste time taking another powerful thrust that left me breathless instantly. Or three other which made my lungs feel like they collapsed. I dug my blunt nails into his biceps "Oh fuck me, don't stop please."

"Like that huh?" he breathed into my ear resuming his usual practice or dirty talk. "I'm gonna wreck you so bad you won't walk tomorrow. Gonna fuck you so hard you'll never want anyone else." My mouth curved into an O shape when he hit my prostrate, unable to make a single sound. It was that good. "This ass is mine."

"Yours." I muttered since there was nothing else my lips could produce. He continued thrusting into mercilessly like there was no tomorrow. There was nothing sweet or slow about this; just complete fucking and utter wreckage and I loved every second of it.

"That's it. Hit me right there." I moaned as Axel abused my prostrate over and over again. He kept on grunting and muttered words like "Mine" and "So good" in my ear. I clutched to his back clawing as hard as I could.

Normally I'd feel bad about it but the pleasure was too much for me to focus on anything else.

"Shit I'm coming!" I wailed as the spurts of white come flew on mine and Axel's chests. Axel took three more thrust before groaning and coming inside the condom. He collapsed on my chest taking a few deep breaths before rolling off me so as not to crush my body with his larger frame. I closed my eyes trying to come down from the high that mind blowing sex like that provided.

I placed my head on his bicep inhaling his sweat mixed with cologne scent "So, am I better than anyone you've ever brought up here?"

He sighed "Shut up Kendall."

*****

"You like The Spinners?" I asked in disbelief as I surveyed his collection of vinyl's in his bedroom shelf. I was dressed in a grey Nirvana tee I borrowed from Axel and my black boxers from before.

"Stop touching those. They're antiques." Axel scolded coming from the bathroom. I rolled my eyes dropping the record back in its place "I'm just surprised. I never really took you for the vinyl's kind of guy."

When I turned to face him he was dripping wet and drying his hair with a towel "In my spare time I like to listen to a few."

"Cool. I love Nat King Cole." I exclaimed turning back to survey his collection. I walked back to the bed and plopped my lean frame on it "Are you ordering take out?"

"Yeah. Does Chinese sound good?" Axel asked dropping his towel on the floor and wearing a pair of clean boxers. I shrugged "Sounds good." And I leaned back shamelessly admiring his toned body. Today I had seen a side of me that I never even knew existed. That was the first time I acted so desperate and needy for sex. I mean I liked sex like every other normal human being out there but for a while I'd maintained that I could live without it if I needed.

Sleeping with Axel had broken every single barrier I had set up and it seemed like I would go crazy if I didn't have more. Thus, the two extra rounds we had before showering I thought cheekily to myself.

"If you keep looking at me like that again you're going to find yourself back on your knees very soon." He bemusedly interrupted my thought train.

I shrugged "Doesn't sound like a bad thing really."

"I'm pretty sure that you would like to walk back to your apartment tomorrow." He winked making my insides contract. I hummed leaning back on a pillow "So am I the only one?"

"The only one what?" he asked obviously bewildered.

I pressed my lips together "The only one that you've brought up to your apartment."

He stopped running his fingers through his hair too look at me and for a moment I panicked hoping that I hadn't gone too far this time. "Yes. Actually."

"Oh." His response surprised me. I remembered what Martin said but it seemed weird for Axel to actually confirm it himself.

He picked up his phone from the small bedside lamp "I'm a very private man. I don't like giving people more space than they deserve." There was surely a double meaning to that.

"And I don't share." He repeated with the same vigour from that day I first met him.

"Hmm." I moved up my leg slowly on the bed. That didn't exactly answer my question but I didn't push further into it.

"I'm pretty sure many people would take offense to that. You being the dashing and irresistible wealthy business man." I teased lightly. He scoffed "There's much more bullshit in the business world that you would ever see."

"How did you even get into business anyway?" I bit my lip.

Axel continued typing away on his phone "It belongs to my father actually." Family business. "When he stepped down he gave all his shares to me, thereby giving me enough power to be elected CEO." So that was what he meant by he owned half of the company. His and his father's shares combined together.

"And your mom?" he stopped typing.

"No more questions please."

I knew when to stop. Axel obviously didn't want to venture into that topic so I gave it to him to respect his privacy on the matter. It's not like we were boyfriends or anything but that didn't stop me from wanting to know more about him. He was as frustrating as a tightly shut cookie jar.

We both stayed in silence until he dropped his phone back on the drawer.

"As long as you're with me I'm sure we'd both expect some sort of openness to each other. But at the same time boundaries need to be respected." He said to me slowly switching to his business-no nonsense tone.

I nodded slowly "I understand."

"Good."

But I couldn't help but feel some sort of dread towards when he said as long as we were together. As if there would be some kind of expiration date to this. That thought shouldn't have made my stomach grumble the way it did.

*****

When I woke up the next day Axel was gone. The bed felt cold and beside me was a single note explaining that he had a meeting early and my name was placed on the list of those allowed up to his apartment.

I couldn't help but feel the sudden disdain that crawled into my chest. It almost felt like he was deliberately running. From what I had what idea even though there was a voice in my head telling me that I did. There was toast and coffee on the breakfast bar but I ignored it only taking a shower before leaving the penthouse.

During the bus ride I felt angry and sad at the same time wondering how on earth I'd gotten back here. Closed off Axel was so annoying. I understood that maybe it was a pretty sad or sensitive topic but it didn't give him the right to act like I'd committed a crime. When I got back to my flat I felt unusually tired and decided to skip a few lectures today and rest myself since I had been working a lot this past week.

The door was opened surprisingly since Pierce was supposed to be at a lecture right now.

I got inside and carelessly dropped my bag on the floor wanting to flop on my bed and curse at Axel till I passed out.

Only I got the greatest shock of my life.

On my couch was seated my sister Mara cross-legged like she'd been waiting for me.

"Hello little brother." Her smile was as wicked as I'd remembered.

Who asked for a cliffy? Hehehe ;)

Chapter 10 - Family Ties

This chapter may contain triggers of abuse and other things so be warned.

"Surprised? Don't I get a hug?" Mara asked as if she were genuinely surprised.

"How did you get in here?" I asked as coldly as I could. She stood up walking towards me "Through the door my little dumbass brother. What are you learning in university at all?" her tone was mocking. I shook my head "Did Pierce let you in?"

She folded her arms across her chest "Oh the little blonde indie boy? Ha he didn't even ask to call you or anything. Practically welcomed me with open arms once I said that I was your sister. These Brits should really give their kids the stranger danger lesson more often." She mused.

"What are you doing here Mara?" I tried to ignore the tremblingly in my voice. Mara smiled "I missed you."

"Go to hell."

She smirked "But don't forget that I vacation there. Besides you weren't taking my calls so mom suggested I come down and see you. I passing by to France so I thought I'd stop here since my flight is much later."

"I have nothing to say to you so please drop this act." I told her "Don't destroy what's beginning to go solid for once in my life."

Her fake smile turned into a sneer "Shut up! You think you deserve anything good huh?!" she yanked my hair and pushed me to the wall. I felt disgusted by myself, that I was weak enough to be overpowered by my own sister. I fought the pain and pretended that I wasn't afraid. But Mara could smell the fear since that was what she fed on. My fear.

"Were you out with another boy hmm?" she asked so softly it scared me more. Mara let go of me and I slid down to the floor still not facing her.

"Do you like it when the boys touch you? Answer me!" She slapped me so hard I heard the ringing in my ears.

A lump formed in my throat "I'm sorry." It wanted to cry but I couldn't give her that satisfaction of breaking me completely. It's pathetic that after all these years and there was no single time I didn't lose to her.

"I know." She stroked my hair "I'm sorry too. All these years tolerating you since you were a child. I should have killed you when you were a child you know? Saved everyone the hassle, especially dad." I fought the burn prickling behind my eyeballs when she mentioned my father.

"I'm glad he's dead now. Although it would have been nice for you to join him sooner." How could she say that so devoid of emotion for the man who loved her since she was a little girl? It enraged me because she had no right to refer my father like that. "But we can't all have what we want can we?"

"I hate you Mara." I choked not trusting myself to say anything else. Mara made a clicking sound with her tongue "Feeling's mutual darling."

She stood up straight and patted down her auburn hair "I hate what this English weather does to my hair." I hated that despite all Mara was beautiful. Her oval face, curved body and impeccable figure made her attractive to almost everyone she came across. But it was so that the most beautiful vessels held bitter poison and that's exactly what Mara was.

Bitter poison.

She turned to me still crouched on the floor "I'll be sure to tell mom about how lovely and warm you were when I visited. Make sure you do the same when she calls."

I didn't reply.

Mara tilted her head "Why don't you ever fight me back Kendall? You know that's one of the things that infuriate me; you never fight me back no matter what I do." She sighed shaking my head "Fate must have done wrong sending me a coward of a brother."

I refused to give in to the burning fear in my chest.

"But you deserve this because it's all your fault." Mara inspected her nails "If only you'd been normal we would still be a happy family. Dad would still be with us. Why couldn't you be normal?"

The guilt consumed me. There would always be that voice deep within the walls of my mind that reminded me that it was my fault.

"But no, you just had to be gay and destroy everything our family worked so hard to build." Her tone went darker. "All I wanted was for us to be a perfect little family. But why couldn't you let us Kendall?"

I shut my eyes tight trying to bounce off her words. But they stuck like Velcro ravishing my insides with every chance they had.

"Please do remember that you'll never deserve anything good in your life." was the last thing she said kissing my cheek before exiting the flat.

I just laid there on the floor without moving, barely even breathing. My sides ached and slow, quiet tears betrayed themselves from my pupils. This was proof that no matter how much I ran, the pain of the past would come back to haunt me.

A sibling was supposed to love and care for their brother or sister without fault. Instead I got a sister who wished I was dead every moment even though I'd done nothing but love her with everything within me growing up.

I just laid there without moving, each of Mara's words replaying in my mind in painfully vivid detail.

*****

Pierce met me that way when he came home which was a few hours later. He freaked out like expected and tried to ask me why the hell I'd been lying on the floor. I tried to wave it off and lied that I'd drank some vodka on the way home and I was pissed out.

I knew he couldn't smell any alcohol in my breath but didn't question any further which I was immensely grateful for.

"Hey um your sister was looking for you today. Well some lady who claimed to be your sister." Pierce said when I was safely tucked in my bed.

"Oh um she left. Just wanted to say hello." I mumbled fisting my comforter. He looked like he wanted to say something else but asked "You sure you're ok mate?"

"Hmmmm." I hummed without looking up.

"Ok." He left my room after hovering by the door a little bit. I remembered when I was younger and Mara had starting this, she made a point to tell me that if I said anything to anyone it would end badly. I was a lot younger then.

Now even at my age I couldn't bring myself to say anything.

Over the years I'd come to realize that telling someone might be the end to the shaky stability my family had. My mother had lost her husband; her son was gay and frowned upon by half of her family members. Mara was the only one who brought any remote joy to our family. Class valedictorian, head of the debate society, dating the richest and most popular boy in high school, getting into Stanford etc. her achievements crowned her the perfect daughter and child doted upon by everyone.

I was just the quiet one in the background not bothered by it all. No one took notice of me except from my mother. I knew she cared about me but sometimes I knew it just seemed easier to love Mara. I didn't blame her; Mara was perfect and smart and god-sent. I was never mad when mom would compare me her sometimes asking why I didn't have any friends or why I got a B when I was capable of getting an A+.

Mind you she never pushed me or made me feel pressured but I knew she wanted me to be more like my older, blameless sister. I could never ignore the way her face always lit up whenever Mara came home with a new award or A+ on some test. It would be selfish for me to take that away from her, so every blow and insult was worth it if my mother got to smile again.

For the remainder of the day a part of me was scared that Mara would come back. This was the first time I'd seen her in months. The last time I saw her was during Christmas last year in our grandparents when she introduced everyone to her fiancé Ivan and gushing about how they would get married during autumn the following year. They had been dating from high school and he was very rich seeing as his family had been hoteliers for a long time. She didn't come on to me much during the day since she was busy shoving her diamond engagement ring in everyone's face. But the nights were a different story.

It was funny that I didn't know why my sister hated me so much. I knew she blamed me for a lot of things, resented me for being gay, but I never figured out why she hated me enough to do all she did. I'm sure it ran a lot deeper than she exposed. The only clue I had was that everything started as soon as dad died.

My phone rang but I let it go to voicemail. My mother left a message saying how happy she was that Mara dropped by and that she was glad we were getting along again.

Axel called making my breathing dishevelled for a little while but I ignored him. He wasn't the only one who had issues at the moment even though I was itching to pick up the phone and answer him. The incident in the morning left me emotionally drained.

So I ignored my ringing phone and slept off, wiping my tears even in my sleep.

******

A week later and I still wasn't picking Axel's calls. I buried myself in unnecessary coursework, even though I was fairly ahead. My mental scars were still freshly from Mara's visit and I didn't have the energy to face Axel yet since he was clearly displeased with me during our last meeting. There was no denying that I missed him or thought about him but at the moment it was better I didn't face him.

So on Thursday night I was surprised to hear a knock on my door. Pierce was out getting laid and was respectful enough not to sexile me from our apartment. Plus he mentioned something about his current fling supposedly having a wonderful water bed.

"Coming." I shouted closing my laptop and leaving it on the couch.

I opened the door cautiously only to discover that it was Axel, deadly suit and all.

"What are you doing here?" I ask genuinely baffled.

"You weren't answering your phone Kendall. I've been worried all week!" I sensed the annoyance in his voice.

I leaned by the door "Well sorry about that. I've been a bit under the weather." I was lying but hopefully he would buy it.

"Was your arm amputated? I don't see why you couldn't pick a single one of my calls." He questioned further. I blew out air "Look I'm fine now so you don't need to tear your head out. Thanks for dropping by."

I tried to close the door but Axel placed his foot "I'm not going anywhere until you tell me the truth about why you've been ignoring my calls."

"God the fucking earth doesn't revolve around you Axel." I snapped "I needed some time to myself is all sheesh."

Axel was silent.

"Open this door now or so help me I'll break it down myself."

His commanding voice captivated me for a second that I didn't know when I let go of the door and allowed him in. it felt weird to have Axel in my apartment.

He made it feel smaller than usual, probably because of his domineering, larger-than-life aura. I folded my arms across my chest facing him "What do you want?"

"I want you to honestly, without stuttering, tell me what happened to you." Ugh, why did he care so much?! Wasn't it obvious enough when I lied that I didn't want him knowing about whatever was going on? But no Axel just had to be so darn stubborn.

I stared at him "Axel it's nothing"-

"You should know by now that I hate lies." He stated. I sighed "It's just some family trouble. Nothing you need to worry about."

"Are you sure?" he asked further.

"Fuck, yes!" I raised up my hands in exasperation. "Now please respect my boundaries the way you obviously want me to respect yours." In a way that was probably a low blow. I was still angry at him for being angry at me because I was just curious so I was using it to drive away his curiosity.

Axel sighed "Look I'm sorry for barging into your business like that."

I nodded weakly "It's cool."

He hesitated for a minute "I was worried about you." if that didn't spring a whole herd of butterflies loose in my stomach I don't know what. He eyed me carefully.

"Um thanks?"

My heart sped as he strode towards me placing his hand on my cheek. His lips pressed to mine in a slow, careful kiss. This was new.

Axel hardly kissed me. Maybe he'd done so a few times after we'd had sex but never a carefree or spur of the moment thing. That's what made this different. After a while the kiss got heated, leading me wrap my hands around his neck. His hands roamed around my body gripping my waist closer to his body.

My body was quite……feminine. I wasn't so girly or anything but that was the best term to describe myself sometimes. I wasn't a twink (curse that derogatory term), but my body was thinner and a lot shaper than most guys. I guess that automatically labelled me a bottom in my last two relationships. I'd topped once, but I shamelessly admitted that I enjoyed bottoming better.

I'll never admit why then.

But with Axel I enjoyed the way he took charge and dominated me. When we were together it was an unspoken rule I went with. It baffled me somehow how eager I was whenever he commanded me or how I always waited till he gave instruction. Somehow being dominated made me feel safe, in a non-disturbed way that is.

"Do you still want me to leave?" Axel asked now peppering kisses on my throat.

"No stay. But just hold me please?"

I was nervous at my suggestion. As much as I wanted to climb him like a tree all the time right now I just wanted him to hold me. But I didn't know how he would react to that.

"Ok."

His answer relived me. We both sat on my tacky couch with my face buried in his chest, inhaling his Armani. This was a complete U turn from the direction I expected us to head tonight. He would come over, we would argue then he would leave pissed off at me.

Not with me curled into him like a baby koala.

"I'll stay until you fall asleep." He murmured to my temple. This man was such an enigma, so layers I was yet to observe within him. Even when my intention was purely to put him off so I could be alone, because I couldn't bear to fall down at his feet again. Yet here I was in his arms but I couldn't shake off the feeling that this was where I wanted to be.

Hey guys sorry if this chapter turns out to be shit. Believe me this was super hard for me to write so don't take it personally if my writing isn't so good.

And I want to bring to everybody's attention that yes, males can be abused and it's completely stupid for anyone to think otherwise. Physical and emotional abuse applies to every gender without execption so no ignorant comments please.

xxxx

Chapter 11 - If The Shoe Fits......

"You've got holes in your jeans, and a fuel in your heart. You don't know what it means to me, to watch you fall apart."

"Kendall." I felt my body being shaken gently.

I slowly peeled my eyes open to see Axel gazing at me intently. I blinked sleepily "Axel?"

I forgot that I had asked him to stay with me and somehow fell asleep along the line. My arms were wrapped around his neck while one of his was buried in my hair tugging at it gently. I was lying with my head on his chest and the rest of my body tucked into his due to the compactness of the couch.

"You were crying in your sleep." He stated. I sniffed suddenly realizing that my face was wet and that his chest was glistening. He had taken off his suit and clothes folding them neatly on the coffee table because it didn't make sense to sleep in a thousand pound suit.

"Sorry about that." I apologised feeling embarrassed about getting snot all over his chest.

"What's wrong Kendall?" He asked sounding both worried and exhausted. I sighed burying my face in the crook of his neck "I'll tell you in the morning please."

He made a sound of discontentment but decided not to say anything else.

"What time is it?" I asked after a while.

"A little past midnight."

"Thank you for staying with me." I murmured into his neck. He ran his hand on my back in a comforting manner "I really wish you would tell me what the problem is. I'd do anything to help."

Oh Axel please don't taunt my heart like this. I'm already beginning to feel more for you than I should. All your shows of care and affection are only making this worse. There was no denying that I felt a lot for Axel more than I did in the beginning and somehow that scared me. As much as I wanted to assure myself that this was just harmless infatuation for the attractive man I was sleeping with, this was much deeper than that.

But it wasn't clear to me yet.

The next time I woke up I was lying alone on the couch swaddling with my baby blue blanket. It was at least 7 by now and the clothes on the coffee table were gone sending me into a mild frenzy until I heard shuffling in the kitchen.

The sweet scent of coffee snuck into my nostrils and I smiled to myself. Pierce doesn't drink coffee.

"I see you're awake." His dreamy voice slowly swayed me into full consciousness.

"Sure am now." I sat up on the couch accepting the mug of steaming coffee from Axel who was dressed up impeccably in his suit. "Thanks for the coffee."

"You don't have a coffee maker so I had to do it regular." I wanted to laugh at the way he said it. Like it was some kind of crime against for not having a fancy espresso maker or something. I sipped "Guess you have to go now."

Axel hummed sitting beside me "I'm still expecting an explanation for what happened last night."

My chest contracted a little "Look I'll be able to tell you sometime. Just... ..trust me I'll tell you someday. But for now please just leave it ok?"

It was obvious Axel wasn't happy with my answer. It's not like you could blame the guy seeing as I sobbed in my sleep nearly giving him a heart attack without any explanation. If I was honest his concern was refreshing and totally did not make me cheese over like a hormonal teen girl inwardly.

"Today I'm going to call you and if your phone rings one second further I'm coming down to take you wherever you are, do I make myself clear?" He said sternly.

I nodded meekly "Yes Axel."

"I'll call you ok?" His tone was softer now as he caressed my cheek. I pecked his lips lightly not wanting to betray my morning breath. All this this sudden affection was surprising but definitely not unaccepted.

After a little more kissing, Axel finally left to go to work and Pierce came in not long after.

"Your boyfriend better borrow me some that mojo he's got." He said taking off his jacket and throwing it on the couch. I raised an eyebrow "Why?"

"Because all week I've been trying to get you out of your PMS mood but he just spends one night and you look like a happy bride."

I blushed "There's no mojo dude."

"Fine. But I'm glad you aren't sulking anymore." Pierce said seriously. I shrugged "Guess I just kind of got over it."

"Or Mr. Vogue screwed it out of your system." He suggested with a cheeky smile.

"Shut up!"

******

For the rest of the day I was in a pretty good mood. Axel kept his promise and managed to text and call me as soon as he could. Considering that the man was also busy I'd say it was pretty considerate of him. That might have kept me smiling all day like an idiot.

But my happiness was short-lived when I came out of the Humanities block to see my sister waiting in a body hugging dress and heels, ignoring the numerous eyes ogling her. My heart dropped for a bit but I managed to walk to her and confront her about what she wanted.

"What are you doing here?" I hissed.

She patted her hair "I'm leaving in two hours and I wanted to let you know." She seemed particularly jumpy or nervous whichever one. But something had obviously made her uneasy.

"And your phone managed to burn in those deadly flames you produce?" I asked sarcastically.

Mara gave me a sharp look "Don't start with me. Mom's been asking me about why your mood's foul every time she calls so next time she does;

you're going to tell her that we had a great time together and what not and that there's nothing wrong with you. And if anyone comes asking about me you didn't see me ok."

"You want me to tell two separate lies? Give me one good reason why I should do anything for you." I folded my arms across my chest.

"Because I said so little brother." she placed her hands on her hips trying to exert her hold on me.

"Last time I checked your word isn't law so you'll have to give me a better reason." I snapped at her. Her face showed some surprise "You don't want to mess with me Kendall. Remember the things I could do to you in a snap. I'll always be able to get you."

She quickly jumped into her rental car and drove away leaving me to process her words. I was tired of being afraid and running from Mara all through my life but her words got me for a moment. My sister was capable of a lot of things I knew, but it worried me to think that she might be capable of doing other things I had no idea about.

That thought haunted me and I tried not to think about it when I was with Axel in his apartment later that night.

"What's on your mind this time?" He asked when we were curled on his couch with my head on his lap.

I shuffled so that I was lying on my back and facing him directly "Nothing. Just coursework and annoying professors is all."

Axel stroked my hair "You're a smart lad. You'll get through it."

I groaned "Please do not ever call me a lad again. That is just too ridiculously English for me to deal with."

"What?" Axel sounded confused in that ridiculously hot accent of his "What do you want me to call you then? Dude?"

I laughed at his expression "If the shoe fits."

"Kendall I'm not calling you dude." He deadpanned.

"Ok fine." I pouted silent for a while. "Wouldn't even fit you anyways."

"Excuse me?"

"I mean you're much too old." I said with a half grin then yelped when I was suddenly rolled and Axel was on top of me pinning my hands above my head "Are you calling me old?"

"Unless there's someone else in this room as ancient but also ridiculously good-looking." I winked.

He huffed "That mouth of yours. I'm not even thirty yet you little minx. Besides eve if I was old I'd still be able to fuck you to submission." How dare he?! He knew fairly well that saying things like that was like setting a matchbox next to a gas tank. High inflammable.

Axel proceeded to kiss down my lips chastely "Like this." He grinded himself on my thigh and oh the gods, it took all within me not to let my eyeballs roll inside my head. This was foul play to the fullest. I sat up pulling him a long with me so that I was sitting on his lap "Hmm that's nice."

"Told you." he muttered peppering more kissing on my collarbone then neck.

"I like it." I purred.

"Good." He muttered before closing the small gap with his lips. The kiss was slow and dirty; exactly my favourite type of kiss. I straddled his lap pushing him closer by the nape of his neck and enjoying the way his arms roamed around my body. I tilted my neck backwards, giving him more leverage to inflict whatever marks he so desired.

I started grinding my crotch against his, causing him to swear and hold my hips tighter.

"Don't do that or I'll come now." He warned.

I managed a sloppy grin "Old man."

I'm sure he was about to retaliate if it wasn't for his obnoxious Blackberry ringing. I hide my disappointment when he leaned over to pick it up.

"Yes?" his answer was sharp and straight to the point. I remained on his lap with my arms around his neck though I shifted back a little because I didn't want to seem rude and listen in on his conversation.

"Lauren why are you calling me?" at the mention of a female name my senses heightened. Not obvious since I didn't him to think that I was interested in his conversation. But that was a big fat lie since I wanted to know who this Lauren female was but I shuffled off his lap anyway.

Axel's expression remained neutral during his conversation with a few "I see's" and "Not right away". Finally he dropped his phone looking less than enthusiastic.

"Anything wrong?" I asked tentatively.

He shook his head "No just a friend calling."

"Ok." I muttered going back to sit on his lap. We didn't kiss anymore; we just sort of settled back into our comfortable intimacy together.

But I couldn't help but wonder why Axel was lying to me.

Sorry that this is short guys. I'm not feeling my greatest right now so I tried to pluck this chapter from the top of my head. I'll try to make the next chapter a lot longer xxx

Chapter 12 - Lies That Bind Part 1

Pain. The unending pain was the first thing I felt on waking up. The beeping sounds around me slowly dragged me back to consciousness. I felt heavy, like my body had become a bag of cement overnight. But the one thing that I couldn't keep up with was the pain. The putrid stench of disinfectant and dread made me know immediately that this was a hospital.

"Shit he's awake." I heard a familiar voice.

There were feet shuffling around and frantic voices but I couldn't make them out individually.

"Kendall, Kendall can you hear me?"

I gently fluttered my eyes open "Axel?"

"It's alright babe. I'm here now, I'm here for you." he soothed gently. And for the first time since waking up something seemed to finally make sense.

48 hours earlier

My bones were aching. It was bad enough that I spent the entire day at the library finishing not one, but two reports but I also did a pop quiz that drained the energy out of me completely. There was nothing I wanted more than to fall into bed and sleep for a billion freaking years. But alas fate was not on my side as I had to stop and help Pierce pick up something from a friend of his in the dorms.

At the end of the day I was completely discouraged from sleeping and decided to hit the local Starbucks for a boost.

I ordered a tall cup of Vanilla Bean, sipping the sweet hot coffee as I wrestled my way out of the shop.

My plan was to go straight home and rest up before waking up for some more zombie-like reading. But my plans were deterred when I bumped into the person I wanted absolutely nothing to do with.

"Shit can you watch where the fuck you're going?! This jacket costs more than your bloody existence!" Jerry shouted pushing my roughly. It was no secret that his family was on the wealthy side since he so generously broadcasted it. I guess they were bankers or something.

It was a good thing that only a little bit of my coffee spilled away but not on Jerry. I guess he didn't care about that little detail.

"I'm sorry jeez it was an accident." I tried to apologize.

Jerry looked irritated "You're lucky seeing as you wouldn't even be able to afford the bloody dry-cleaning." I tried not to roll my eyes at that.

"I'm sorry." I tried one more time being the more sensible one.

"Stupid fag." I'd like to say that his words stung and made me feel bad. But the truth was that I already had my fair share if insults and homophobic slurs that the only thing I could do now was the close my eyes and think about better things which mattered to me. "It's not like I expect anything less from a bloody cocksucker."

"Your problem not mine." I muttered moving to the bus stop without a single glance back.

A part of me hoped that he would remain there still spewing insults and appearing as a bigger idiot than normal. But the more mature part of me had forgotten about it in a second.

When I got back to the complex I noticed the black town car parked in front, looking so out of place in my tacky block of flats. I rolled my eyes walking to the car and tapping at the window. It rolled down immediately to reveal a questioning Axel.

"Wanna explain to me why you're parked out here like a stalker?" I asked in an exasperated tone.

"I was coming to take you out for dinner but someone doesn't seem very grateful." Axel sighed like it was the most logical thing in the world to say.

"And a simple call telling me that you'll be here wouldn't have sufficed? You just had to camp outside in the dark like some weirdo?" I asked with a raised eyebrow.

"You weren't picking up your phone." He said accusingly at me. I frowned bringing out my phone from my pocket "But you didn't ca-"

5 missed calls from Axel. Oh shit.

With my mood today I've barely looked at my phone for anything other than time today.

"Sorry." I mumbled ignoring his slight glare. The door opened for me to enter "Come on we don't have all day."

I sighed "Let me just drop my stuff and change my clothes at least."

Axel shook his head "We have only 20 minutes to get to our reservation." What? But I couldn't go anywhere looking like this. I have a little spot of vanilla bean on my shirt for goodness sake. But the look he gave me clearly showed he didn't want any more argument so I resigned to my fate and got into the car.

There go my plans of infinite sleep but I'm not complaining so much.

******

I tried not to let my scowl show while watching Axel read the menu. Sure enough we were in Chez Bonne, a fancy restaurant and it didn't help that I looked like someone from failed contestant on Wipeout. I had my black Rolling Stones tee with jeans and a faded green hoodie. Nothing fit for a place like this.

Axel looked impeccable as always in a three piece suit without a single wrinkle even though I knew he was coming straight from work. It's like he could put multiple hours into working and not even break a single sweat. Somehow I didn't blame the waitress for swooning when she thought we weren't looking. It was a general effect I guess.

"So what's the occasion?" I asked dropping my menu on the table.

"How so?"

I shrugged "You just took me out without warning. There must be some occasion or reason." Even though I had been with Axel for almost three weeks now this man was far from predictable.

"Do I need a reason to want to take you out?" He asked seriously sipping his wine.

I bit my bottom lip "Well everything happens with reason."

He nodded "Well I felt like taking you out. That's my reason." I think he's infuriating on purpose sometimes. For once why can't he give me an answer that isn't in cryptic message? Ugh!

The waitress came and took out orders bringing our food only a few minutes afterwards. I silently ate my steak while Axel seemed pretty occupied with his phone. People were giving us looks, particularly me, but I was too tired to care and he was too occupied to notice.

"Are you doing anything tomorrow?" He asked suddenly without looking away from his phone.

I chewed thoughtfully "I'm not sure. I'm supposed to email my essay to my professors by then since I'll be too tired to do so this night but I don't think I have any attendance compulsory lectures though."

"Good." Axel sipped his wine "I'm taking you somewhere by noon."

"Where?" my curiosity was spiked like a little kid.

His mouth twitched "It's a surprise." I tried my best not to pout because that wouldn't be manly. Hmm he seemed pretty attentive this past week entertaining me in his penthouse. We weren't only having sex; sometimes we'd just order in and make out hotly, or watch movies together. In fact a little while ago I just discovered that he was a huge Star Wars fan.

Who would have guessed?

I chuckled silently remembering the devious glare he shot me when I said that Anakin was kind of tacky. Honestly I did enjoy the changes immensely it's just that they made me wonder where we were heading. That part confused me.

It's not like we were boyfriends or anything. Actually when I thought about it I really didn't know what we were since we hadn't put a label on things yet. All that I knew was that we fucked and hung out sometimes. I'd say we were fuck buddies, but that wouldn't feel right. Something within made me feel like this was deeper than some no-strings-attached relationship.

But yet we weren't in a serious commitment that like.

"Penny for your thoughts."

I scoffed "They'd be worth a thousand at least."

Axel drummed his fingers on the table "Kendall what's bothering you?"

I stabbed my food a little harder than necessary "Nothing's wrong with me. I just had an annoying day."

His expression told me that everything I said was 100% bullshit but he said nothing.

"Axel!"

I looked up to see a beautiful woman approaching our table in a tight dress. There was no mistaking this; she was gorgeous. Her hair was pulled up in a neat French bun that exposed her lovely collarbones and shoulders. She was on the heavy side, boob wise. I'm gay doesn't mean that I don't notice obviously huge melons. I'm not blind.

Her dress flaunted her killer curves as she swayed to our table, eyes set on Axel like laser beams. He swore under his breath "What are you doing here?"

She frowned but only for a second "I called you this afternoon but you told me that you were working late and couldn't meet up. I'm meeting with a friend shortly."

Interesting, I had no idea that I was work. Unless you count in some aspects.

Axel clenched his teeth "That wasn't any of your business and I told you that I couldn't meet up not specifically that I was working." Cat's already out of the bag dearie I thought bitterly sipping my wine.

"Oh my manners." She turned to me dramatically "Hi I'm Lauren Axel's ex-fiancée." My entire being went limp.

What.

The.

Fudging.

Hell.

I looked slowly at Axel who was deliberately not looking my way with a scowl imprinted on his face. I thought he was gay?! But he didn't seem like the closet type and-

"Lauren we were discussing in private if you didn't notice." He told her sternly. "I'll see you tomorrow."

Lauren didn't look too happy about that "But if it's your friend we can excuse him-"

The nerve of this bitch!

"Actually we were about to go to his apartment so he could fuck the life outta me but please take your time." I said sweetly. She looked completely shocked while Axel maintained his calm façade but anyone could see the surprise there. I don't know what came over me but it was definitely strong enough for me to forget to filter my words.

"Well then...." She dragged not seeming to keen on my presence anymore "I'll see you tomorrow Axel."

He didn't even reply as she sashayed away.

"I don't know about you, but I'm pretty full now." I said as normally as I could. He just sighed and asked for the cheque.

When Timothy brought the car around neither of us said anything. I pretended to occupy myself with my phone checking up on social media and articles that didn't concern me. I had every right to get angry, he lied and made me look stupid in front of his supermodel fiancée. The most intriguing part was that I thought he was gay. Did he lie about that too?

"Kendall-"

"It's fine I'm just a friend." I said with a hint of resentment. Axel sighed eyeing the front "It's not what it seemed. If I knew she was going to be there-"

"You'd have picked a better lie is that it?" my voice was getting louder.

"Fuck she's my ex Kendall, do you expect me to announce her name every time we talk?" he snapped at me.

I was taken aback "When I was at your place and she called and you lied saying it was a friend. Obviously you guys weren't very broken up."

"Don't even start with that." He threatened. "Or would you like me to remind you about the constant lies you've been telling? You were crying in your bloody sleep but yet you couldn't even muster the courage to tell me the truth."

"That doesn't have anything to do with this!" I shouted.

He cocked an eyebrow "Really? My misdoings are fine for us to talk about but lord forbid we bring up yours."

"They don't have anything to do with us!" I exclaimed. "That's strictly my business."

We stopped at the traffic light. Axel blew out air "We aren't engaged anymore I've told you. Besides I don't know why this affects you so much we're not exclusive or anything." Now that hurt me deep inside like a knife.

"Of course." I said bitterly "I'm just a stupid university kid you've been fucking all this while. Joke's on me." I opened the door and grabbed my bag.

"Where the hell are you going?!" he asked confused.

"I don't stay where I'm not wanted. Go fuck yourself Axel Gold." I slammed the car and walked away without looking back. The walk back home would be long but at least I had my bus card with me reducing the journey.

I couldn't stop the tears from flowing freely. Maybe I was wrong; maybe it was my fault for forgetting the main arrangement. Men like Axel don't date boys like me. It was stupid for me to think that I was someone like me had a chance with him.

He'd never feel the way I felt for him.

Ohhhh trouble in paradise? ;)

This chapter was going to be super long so I had to cut it into part 1 & 2. So when the next chapter comes you guys will have to read them like they're one chapter not two seperate ones.

Gosh I hope that wasn't confusing xxxx

Chapter 13 - Lies That Bind Part 2

"Forget about him Kenny. That asshole isn't worth your time anyway." Pierce said fiercely sucking the life out of his cherry Italian soda. "Anyone who could let you walk without a glance doesn't deserve your spectacular ass, even if he is rich enough to put the Royal family to shame."

I rolled my eyes "Thank you for your compulsory best friend bashing of my ex but it wasn't really necessary. I'm fine."

He snorted "The hell you are." He was right. I wasn't fine at all. Last night I cried all the way back to my apartment trying to wrap my head around the events which took place. Pierce was there waiting in front of the TV and so I cried in his lap all night like a little kid. My reaction might have been slightly baffling considering the nature of our relationship but I didn't care. I missed Axel even if I also hated him at the same time. That was the aspect that drove me absolutely crazy.

Part of me knew that I was being irrational but I couldn't bring myself to care. I didn't lie to Axel; I just blandly refused to tell him what was going on. But he lied right to my face which is not ok and on top of that made me feel like a freaking hoe.

Yet I couldn't help but subconsciously check my phone for any calls or texts since last night but there were none. Since last night we had zero communication.

I looked outside the window of the ice cream parlour where we were. After my classes Pierce had all but dragged me here to forget all about the situation and convince me that Axel wasn't worth a grain of salt. So far it wasn't working. I just let me gaze wonder around the people until I noticed something.

There was a man on a motorcycle outside. At first I didn't think anything about it but he was there for almost 20 minutes which gave me a sort of uneasy feeling. He wasn't staring at me or anything but even though he looked like he was on the phone I just had this feeling ok? Maybe it was a stupid instinct or fear but I was allowed to be paranoid every once in a while.

I forced myself to look away and sighed "Look I'm fine. It's not like we were really serious anyway." That revelation left a bitter taste in my tongue.

He sighed "But you obviously liked him more than you let one."

I didn't reply instead I sucked my banana milkshake intensely until I had to stop to take a breath. I wasn't going to talk about that no matter what. In fact I wouldn't even think about it one bit. Whatever my feelings were, they were completely irrelevant since my association with Axel was pretty much over at this point.

"Hey." Pierce said softly "You're a good guy Ken-doll so don't take this in too deep. In fact- let's go clubbing! That would be the perfect way to forget this whole ordeal!"

"I'll pass. Not really interested in getting wasted out of my ass again." I muttered.

"No way, you're going clubbing with me and we are going to have a good time and forget all about Axel what's-his-face and pick up some hot guys." He said firmly.

"Or girls." I cheeked.

"Whatever." He brushed clearly trying to avoid what he knew I was insinuating. "It's non-negotiable Kendall."

I rolled my eyes "Fine. But I'll chain to the bar if you even think about ditching me tonight, again."

"Never!"

Martin called me later that day while I was doing my laundry. It was a blessing in disguise that my Pierce's parents didn't mind pooling the money to get their son a washing machine and dryer so none of us had to endure the shame of going to a Laundromat.

"Hello?" I said turning on the dial for cotton.

"Kendall it's Martin." He said and as always I could almost hear the filmy halo of happiness bursting through him.

"Hey Martin how are you doing?" I leaned on the washer.

There was some shuffling at the background "I'm good. Just came back from visiting some other galleries so I thought I'd call you since Axel is being a hardass and won't answer any of my calls."

"Axel and I aren't together anymore." I said quietly wondering if we were ever really together in the sense.

"But why?" Martin asked sounding genuinely confused and a bit sad "That fucker messed up again didn't he?"

"No it was kind of the two of us." I explained nervously. "I guess we weren't just that compatible."

He sighed "Sorry about that. You guys just seemed really good together really." It didn't help that he sounded completely sincere.

"Relax it's not like we were dating or anything. It was just sex." I closed the dryer harder than necessary to punctuate.

"Still I kinda liked seeing you together. It's just you seemed so good for Axel and all."

I switched the washer to rinse "Not good enough. Thanks for calling me Martin but I'd understand of Axel didn't want you calling me anymore."

"Whoa who said anything about that? You're my friend too and if he has a problem with that he can kick it up his arse. Axel's a big boy." He replied with an actual snort.

I couldn't help chuckling "Thanks dude." Gosh it seemed like a guy like Martin could only appear in a golden basket from the gods. There was no way someone could be so perfect and considerate and just plain awesome. Honestly if he wasn't with Spencer and I wasn't so stupidly hung on Axel I might have considered dating him. He's also pretty cute if I might add.

"No problem mate. I'd offer to hang with you but Spencer's coming home soon and we haven't been spending that much time together." I smirked realizing exactly what he was insinuating.

"Don't worry about me but thanks for calling I really do appreciate it." My voice was heavy with gratitude.

"Hey what are friends for?" he laughed.

At least Axel did well by helping me meet someone like Martin.

******

I'm glad that we didn't go to Red Velvet this time. Not because of anything serious but a change of scenery was nice. I hated how Axel and I weren't even in a real relationship yet I was acting like this was a proper break-up with the moping and inner-denial. It annoyed me to bits honestly.

The club we decided to go to was called Chaos and a lot larger than Red Velvet. Their DJ wasn't as good as DJ Spinderella though but their epic bar and space made up for it. Pierce wanted to stay with me at the bar but I convinced him that I was fine and didn't need babysitting. So in no time he was grinding his ass up to some hunk while I just sipped a beer not wanting to get too drunk in case I had to haul Pierce's wasted butt back home.

"Girl troubles?" the older bartender asked me.

I cocked an eyebrow "What makes you assume I have girl troubles?"

He shrugged "When a guy sits lonely at a bar he's either thinking of murder or relationship troubles."

"Not a girl anyway." I mumbled.

"A guy then?" I shot my head up.

"My kid's also gay so I don't really have any problem with it." He explained.

I nodded slowly "It's a guy yeah. But he's like way out of my league anyway so I'm trying not to think about it."

"What makes you think so?" he leaned closer.

"Are we seriously going to do that whole tell a stranger your problems thing?" I questioned. He just laughed and I pursed my lips "Right. He's rich, handsome and all while I'm some lowly university student. We weren't even that serious anyway but he's made it pretty clear that he doesn't want me that way. Old girlfriend showed up and he lied about it."

"I'm not great at the whole Dear Abby thing but I can tell you that when people don't discuss about past relationships it means that they don't want it to become relevant in the current one. What kind of person broods over their ex unless they wanna get back together? None."

He was fairly correct.

"You're pretty young, got your whole life ahead of ya. If this guy doesn't want you, there will always be other guys in the future. But just honestly find out if he didn't tell you about her because he didn't think it was relevant. Or maybe he genuinely forgot about her." He stated.

I bobbed my head "Thanks."

"What's your name kid?"

"Kendall." I replied shaking my beer.

"American aye? My wife's American from Washington." He said with a side smile.

"That's cool, thanks for the advice again dude." I thanked one more time before he went to serve someone else.

Even though the bartender had some air of truth in his words, Axel didn't see me like that. Or at least that was what I convinced myself. There was never really a time I asked him what we were really or if he wanted more. It seemed stupid then - but maybe because I wanted more.

My head is so fucked up.

After an hour of watching people dance I located Pierce and told him that I wanted to go. He didn't even object; he just hopped off the lap of the body builder he was sucking face with and wrapped his arm around my shoulder.

I surely did not miss the daggers the guy sent me for cock-blocking him.

"Shit forgot my wallet inside." He announced once we were outside.

"Seriously?" I gave him an annoyed look.

"Probably left it in the booth. Be right back!" he promised before rushing back inside. I just sighed walking out to the front. There were a couple of smokers so I moved around back to avoid the bitter fumes. It was a bit secluded but I felt a lot better.

Suddenly a gloved hand covered my mouth making me struggle. My assailant was freakishly strong because his grip on my neck chocked me. Another man appeared and surprise, he was the same dude from the ice cream shop.

"Help!" I tried to scream but it earned me a punch in the gut. There were two more punches when I tried to kick and fight my way out of his grip.

"Shut up you stupid kid!" he bellowed. My captor flicked a pen-knife to my throat "Now don't move unless you want me to slice you up."

I stopped moving but the fear radiated from my body nevertheless. The guy from the shop violently yanked me and pushed me on the wall searching my body frantically and tossing away my phone.

I groaned in pain as they dropped me on the ground tying my hands with a strong rope. Next there was a sharp sting on my left arm. It made me feel dizzy and tired at the same time making me to suspect that it was some kind of drug.

"What do you want from me?" I slurred since I was quickly losing my visual senses. The bulker guy grabbed me "Don't rough him up too much else he won't be of much use."

But before he could do anything two bouncers appeared "Aye! Drop the kid!"

A gun sounded and I was dropped roughly on the floor hurting my arm.

"Kendall!"

I felt someone rush up to me shaking my body "Shit, Kendall are you ok? Someone call a bloody ambulance!" I realized then that it was Pierce. My vision was blurry making it hard for me comprehend what was going on around me.

"Mate you'll be fine I promise." He petted my hair but all I could see was darkness.

Present time (From previous chapter's beginning)

Pain. The unending pain was the first thing I felt on waking up. The beeping sounds around me slowly dragged me back to consciousness. I felt heavy, like my body had become a bag of cement overnight. But the one thing that I couldn't keep up with was the pain. The putrid stench of disinfectant and dread made me know immediately that this was a hospital.

"Shit he's awake." I heard a familiar voice.

There were feet shuffling around and frantic voices but I couldn't make them out individually.

"Kendall, Kendall can you hear me?"

I gently fluttered my eyes open "Axel?"

"It's alright babe. I'm here now, I'm here for you." he soothed gently. And for the first time since waking up something seemed to finally make sense. The bright light hurt my eyes but I managed to tentatively open them anyway to see Axel sitting beside me a fearful shadow cast on his handsome features.

I tried to sit up but my ribs hurt like hell making me wince in pain. "Easy, easy." He helped place some pillows on my back so that I was well balanced.

"Hey." He held my hand.

"How did you get in?" I asked still squinting.

"Your roommate called me as soon as they brought you to the A&E. Had to tell the nurses that I'm your boyfriend for them to let me in." Axel replied softly still stroking my hand. At this point I could kiss Pierce on the ass for whatever screw bolt in his head made him call Axel. "He's gone to get some coffee though."

"I'm sorry." His voice was a lot smaller now.

"Me too." I tried to smile but my whole body hurt. "Ribs are on fire."

"The doctor will be here soon but they gave you some morphine for the pain. It's on your IV." He explained. Sure enough there was one attached to my wrist dripping gently into my veins.

"When I got the call I was so scared." He confessed staring deep into my eyes "There's only been one time in my life I was this scared. I was so mad at myself for letting you go that night, like it's the most stupid thing I've ever done. You're not irrelevant, far from it Kendall. Wanted to call you all this while but I thought you were still mad at me."

Huh, guess we were on the same page then.

"But when I got the call I literally dropped everything and came rushing here. Couldn't even stand the thought of having you hurt." His appearance clarified that. Even though I enjoyed seeing Axel in his suits right now he was wearing nothing but a pair of boot cut jeans and a fitted white V neck exposing his sleeve tattoos completely. If I wasn't in utter pain I wouldn't hesitate to jump into the nearest janitors' closet with him.

Even his distorted looked screamed sex appeal.

"I'm sorry for reacting the way I did back in the car." I looked down shamefully. "If you didn't want to tell me about Lauren it was your call. I'm sorry for acting like a spoilt brat."

Axel stroked my cheek "Hey it's fine." He kissed my hands "When you get out of here no more lies ok? We'll be honest with each other."

I nodded shyly "So you would want us to be together?"

"Of course, that is if you want it-"

"Yes!" I didn't care if it hurt. I was going to make it very clear that I wanted to be with Axel solely, no one else.

He smiled really brightly leaning down to kiss me chastely "I missed you so much. Martin called me and gave me the biggest talk off ever."

I groaned "Sorry about that. We just talked a bit."

"It's ok I needed it anyway." Axel assured. Right now even though I was in pain I couldn't be happier. Axel and I were no longer walking in circles around each other; we clearly wanted this together.

"Kenny!" Pierce rushed to my side with two Costa cups in hand "I was so worried and all when I didn't see you! I heard a shout and convinced the two guys outside to help me find you." I could tell that he wanted to hug me but was restraining himself because of my condition.

"Thanks P." I answered with a smile. His eyes darted to Axel for a second "I'll come back later." Cheeky little thing. He waltzed out of the room with an actual spin on his heels. That boy should really stop lying about being Bi, he's as flaming as they get.

"Do you remember what happened?" Axel asked tentatively.

I nodded "I just stepped out back to wait for Pierce since we went clubbing. Then some guys grabbed me and started hitting me. One of them drugged me or something because I started feeling drowsy after. But I guess Pierce found me with some guys on time."

He listened attentively "I'll kill whoever did this to you."

"It was so scary. Why would anyone want to kidnap me?" I asked in a small voice. Axel kissed my cheek "You're good now. I won't let anyone hurt you."

The doctor came moments later with a bulky man and Pierce. He a young Indian man in his forties and a gentle face "How are you feeling now Mr. Ross?"

"Sore." I complained.

"I'll get you some more pain medication." He said sympathetically "You were drugged with a strong sedative and bruised a few ribs but apart from that there's nothing to worry about. In two days you'll be discharged and free to go." He assured.

"Thanks." I managed weakly. The bulky man came to my side "I'm Detective Palin from the London Metropolitan Police and I'm here to collect your statement."

"Excuse me officer but he's not in any position to be interrogated." Axel said.

He nodded "I understand Mr. Gold but this is protocol. I'm sorry. May I ask your relationship with Mr. Ross?" he asked Pierce and Axel.

"We're roommates." He piped.

"And I'm his boyfriend." Oh how I loved that title! A smug smile worked its way to my face despite my state.

"I can answer a few questions." I assured everyone. The detective brought out a pen and pad "What where you doing outside the club Chaos?"

"I was waiting for Pierce to go home. He forgot something inside."

"Did you by any chance have contact with any of the men beforehand?"

I thought hard "I did see one of them in an ice cream shop today but I brushed it off because it didn't seem like he was spying on me."

Pierce swore looking guilty.

He wrote that down "Have you had a falling out with anyone lately? Enough for them to want to harm you."

"No." I said honestly. "Unless it's spilling coffee or something."

"So you've had no other contact whatsoever with them?"

I shook my head.

"Do you have any family or relatives?"

"My mom and her boyfriend live in America. I'm only here for university." I replied.

"Any other family members?" he insisted.

I hesitated glancing downwards "Well I have a sister."

"Do you know where she is?" Detective Palin asked further.

"I-I don't really know."

He cocked an eyebrow "You don't really know where your own sister is?" I felt uneasy all of a sudden as I always did when it came to Mara.

"Detective shouldn't you be looking for the men who did this to him?" Axel stated but I could sense the irrational on his tone. It was obvious that he could sense my uneasiness."

"Well Mr. Gold we have them in custody already. Mr. Ross's statement will be used in court when charging them." He explained.

"Well that's enough for now please." Axel said firmer. He sighed "Well I'll see you gentlemen whenever."

As soon as he left I breathed a sigh of relief. That interrogation made me feel intense. Axel kissed my forehead wrapping his arms around me "It's ok babe you're safe now. I'll protect." Despite what happened I did feel at ease once again just being in his arms.

Wow a complete U-turn right? Anywaysssssssss there is more to come because, if you think the drama's over baby you're mistaken. Haha, don't wanna give too much away xx

P.S Who do you guys think could play Pierce? Comment+Vote

Chapter 14 - Hearts On Fire

I was discharged from the hospital two days later. Axel insisted that I stayed with him until I felt better before I could even think of going back for classes. At first I felt bad leaving Pierce all alone by himself in our apartment but he practically threatened me if I didn't go with Axel. Judging by the devious smirk he was sporting I planned on burning my sheets when I got back because Lord knows the crazy plans he had for my room.

Urgh I felt like puking just thinking about it. Pierce and Axel got along considerably, seeing as he was the 20 year old kid who trashed his boat once.

Martin and Spencer came to visit me the day before I got discharged. Martin was still enthusiastic as ever assuring me that I'd make a speedy recovery while Spencer was concerned about what happened and if there were any legal precautions necessary his firm would take the case pro bono. Everyone's concern was truly touching but the one thing I refused to do was call my mother. Axel tried to convince me but I refused.

I didn't want her to get the impression that something was wrong and come rushing down every single time. However I promised that if the police decided that the men weren't just acting alone then we would call her.

Calling Mara didn't even register once in my mind.

"Please Axel." I begged for what was probably the millionth time.

"No." Axel answered without any consideration. This man! He had told me this morning that he had something he was going to show me but refused to tell me what it was. To make matters worse I was blindfolded and threatened with spanking if I even thought of taking it off. And the latter might have given me happy chills but that's completely out of it.

"Please...." I dragged placing my hand on his lap in a bid to get the information out of him.

I felt him stiffen "Love unless you'd like us to get into a serious car crash, try not to get me hard ok?" I removed my hand with my face obviously burning up because of his words.

He chuckled "Just be patient we're almost there."

I huffed "Well patience is not my fort. Tell me now!"

"It's a surprise."

"I don't like surprises."

"Well you have love." He said taking a turn left. Timothy didn't follow us today making me very glad. He wasn't giving me any "I'll kill you" looks but it felt nice that it was only Axel and I alone this time. Like really alone.

"Just trust me on this one." Axel assured and I leaned back. I could trust, I could trust him right? After a few more minutes we stopped. "Are we here yet?"

"Yes we are." He replied unbuckling his seatbelt. I was about to remove the blindfold "No not yet."

"Come on." I whined quite pathetically. He laughed opening my door for me and helping me get out so I wouldn't fall due to my lack of vision.

"This better be worth it." I stated as Axel's arm snaked around my waist.

"Don't worry it is." He assured. Wherever we were, it was quite sunny. Even through my blindfold I had to squint a little to avoid the unmerciful rays of the sun. Axel placed his hands on my shoulder "Are you ready?"

If it wasn't for the temporary lack of vision I would have glared at him "Are you seriously asking me that?"

He kissed my neck gently dragging the scarf off my eyes "Surprise."

Oh. My. Glorious. Fudge.

Right in front of me was The Silver Phoenix in all her majestic glory, bouncing gently on the water in broad daylight. I turned to him "Axel oh my gosh, are you serious?!"

He shrugged "Seeing as last time you were on it I threatened to kill you I thought that it would be nice for us to have a different set of memories. So do you like it?"

My answer was grabbing him by the head and kissing the hell out of him until neither of us could breathe anymore. He held my waist close to his body until we were left gasping for air "Hmm I like the way you say yes."

"Thank you so much. I mean this was so thoughtful, how did you even?" I interrupted myself by crushing my lips on his again. We were getting pretty frisky already so Axel had to pull away forcefully.

"I'm afraid if we don't get on I might have to make memories here on the docks." He whispered sending delicious shivers down my spine. We moved up the gangplank which was a lot easier than last time seeing as it wasn't night and I wasn't freaking out of my mind.

A tall man in his thirties appeared wearing cargo pants and a Polo shirt "Mr. Gold welcome back."

"Thank you Bill." He greeted "Kendall this is Bill Wagner, Bill this is Kendall my boyfriend." I shook his hand which was unsurprisingly callused for a sailor.

"Nice to meet you." I greeted politely.

"Same." He replied with a brisk smile. "Do you need any help sir?"

"None I'm just going to give Kendall a little tour." Bill nodded and proceeded to the other side of the boat, leaving us alone on the deck.

Axel opened the sliding doors leading me inside the cabin. We moved past the luxurious crème coloured L shaped sofas and the impressively massive window above giving a really cool view of the clear sky. The rest of the cabin was sleek and modern with a plush master cabin and two bathrooms to the right. The galley was to the right with the kitchen.

"Are we sailing?" I asked excitedly plopping myself on the bed of the master cabin.

"Not today sorry." Axel apologized lying right on top of me "But I will go sailing with you sometime yeah?" he brushed my lips with his thumb before pressing a chaste kiss on them.

"Hmmm." I threw my head back "How many people have been here?"

"Just my dad, Spencer and Martin – a couple of other friends too." He replied nonchalantly against my neck. "Not many people but no one's ever been in here before." I knew he meant the bedroom.

"What about Lauren?" I asked deciding to risk it. He stilled for only a second "She didn't like yachts. Said they made her seasick." A small sick rush of pleasure went through me happy that I did something with Axel that she hadn't.

"Don't wanna talk about her now." He muttered kissing my chest through the unbuttoned sections.

I closed my eyes "What about Bill?"

"I told him that we'd be fine. He's gone to the marina for two hours." That was a long time. Hopefully I planned on making good use of it.

Axel unbuttoned the rest of my shirt, pressing kisses all over my stomach and chest while leaving sensual beard burns in his wake. I hummed at every contact running my fingers through his thick gorgeous hair. It was a while since we'd done anything like this, especially since he refused to touch me after I came back from the hospital.

"Skin's like silk." He muttered at my navel licking the little hole and driving me insane. My khakis were pulled around my feet and flung somewhere in no time. All that were left were my grey Mickey Mouse boxers.

"Seriously." Axel shot me an amused glance.

I rolled my eyes "They're comfortable so shut up and don't jud– oh shit!" my member had now disappeared into his mouth and I moaned shamelessly loud for all ears. I hoped Bill was really off the boat.

"So good." He stated making a pop sound before putting my member back in his mouth. My eyes rolled to the back of my head as I made gentle thrusts into Axel's mouth enjoying every single second he blew me like a pro.

"We have a problem." I said breathlessly.

"What is it?" Axel asked sounding worried already. I narrowed my eyes "Why am I the only naked one here?"

He smirked and shook his head "Sorry love."

"I want your clothes off." I had no idea how I sounded so authoritative all of a sudden but with the way Axel's eyes were clouded with lust, I didn't think it was a bad thing.

"As you wish."

He yanked off his LV sweatshirt and sinfully fitted jeans before pressing himself against me in another searing kiss. His tongue dominated my mouth, forcing itself into every corner without resistance from me. He grabbed my thighs grinding himself slowly on my crotch creating that delicious friction we both craved.

I dug my fingers into his back "More please." I didn't want to release this way. I wanted him located properly destroying my insides.

"Foreplay first babe." He whispered making me groan "Then after that I'm going to screw you so fucking hard that they'll hear you in every country."

My body turned to Jell-O at the dirty promise hoping that he would fulfil every last one on me.

Wow, I really am turning slutty.

I blindly dragged his black silk boxers down to his knees while Axel assisted me but kicking them away.

He groaned into my mouth now our bare cocks were rubbing against each other, flipping us over so that I was on top of him. Without breaking away from our kiss he blindly fished for something in the bedside drawer beside us. I was about to question him when he emerged with a bottle of lube.

"Sit up love." He commanded and I heeded biting my bottom lip as he coated my entrance with the cold sticky substance. He stuck two fingers teasing me and I complied bucking my hips with the rhythm of his fingers.

"Fuck Axel." I moaned.

Axel lined my rim with his cock only letting half inside, groaning at the feeling "I'm not even fully in you yet but you're squeezing my cock. So fucking greedy babe."

His English accent + dirty talk = heaven on earth.

"Want you in me, filling me up." I pleaded trying to push further. He eventually complied allowing his member to enter completely making my mouth form into an O shape. It wasn't news that Axel was big but at the moment if felt like I'd shoved the Eiffel tower up my ass.

"Oh God Kendall you're absolutely milking me. Oh shit babe you're fucking tight." He rambled on as bounced tentatively on his cock. A few more slow thrusts and he hit my prostrate - making me cry out like a banshee.

Axel held my thighs in place pushing himself in and out, abusing my prostrate every single time. My palms were placed firmly on his heavily perspiring chest desperately trying to match his every thrust. Our moans and grunts bounced all over the room and radiated back to our bodies as slick heat. Right now it wouldn't matter if the whole world stopped turning, none of us would notice.

His fingers dug into my sides as I rolled my hips in perfect circles making him swear over and over again.

All I could feel was that sexual hunger. The need for him to devour me completely; take me in any way he wished, throbbed through my veins. It was animalistic and intense and for a moment I wondered how this part of me surfaced. Surely it had always existed but nothing ever stirred within me to bring it out.

My last two relationships were average high school romances, nothing to be taken seriously or even thought about. Sure it was with my second boyfriend Theo that I had lost my virginity. The sex wasn't great; sure we explored each other and learned a lot but I was still as almost clueless as a virgin.

Until Axel awoke this dangerous beast inside me. It was insatiable like in an incubus but only stirred every time his skilful hands made contact with my body. And now that I had tasted this rare fruit there was no going back.

He flipped us so that he was on top once again, thrusting into me like a possessed man. I moaned loudly at each contact dragging my blunt nails over his inked biceps. Sweat dripped from his forehead unto my chin dribbling down to my throat which I found oddly erotic.

His lips found their way to my neck, bruising the tender skin mercilessly while I held on and cried out.

"Axel..."

"So close babe." He assured griping my thighs with his iron fist.

Suddenly he thrust in for the last time and a straight shot of cum spilled over our chests making me shout his name while digging my fingers in his back.

At the same time he grunted "Fuck Kendall!" releasing his hot seed inside me completely.

Our heavy breathing was the only sounds heard on the entire boat. It felt like I was only remembering how to breath after an eternity of pleasure.

Axel propped himself on his shoulders so that his weight wouldn't crush me and surveyed me intensely before gently pressing his lips on mine. The kiss was slow and nice, like a nice comforting reminder of all the good things to come.

"I don't think I remember my name." I whispered softly to Axel's chest.

He chuckled putting his arm around my shoulder "What are you trying to say?"

"That you fucked the intelligence out of me asshole." I tried to glare at him but my body was too weak. I wanted to shut off completely for a few hours and thankfully Axel knew this.

"Sleep now. Maybe you'll remember it then." His voice sounded soft and warm and lulled me to sleep immediately.

******

I woke up to the sound of waves crashing. Even though we were still at the docks it was nice to wake up to. I stirred a little, waking Axel up immediately since I was lying with my head on his chest.

"Hey." I said softly.

Axel ran his hand through my hair kissing me chastely "How did you sleep?"

"Really nice." I muttered enjoying the feel of his hands on me. "Thanks for bringing to your yacht. It's really cool."

He kissed my nose "You're welcome babe." The title made my insides bubble. This was the first time he called me babe when we weren't having sex together and it sounded good. The sky was darker meaning we'd been here for some time.

"And thank you for seducing me inside it." He smirked making me slap his arm playfully.

"Old pervert." I said feigning annoyance. He rolled his eyes "Please minx if I were old, then I wouldn't be able to that thing with my hips that makes you scream out."

My face was the colour of pure red wine by now. "Asshole."

Axel hummed staying quiet for only a few minutes before saying "Do you want to know why I left Lauren?"

"You don't have to tell me if you don't want to." I started quickly. "It's fine really."

"I want to Kendall." He stated solidly.

I nodded slowly waiting for him to begin.

He propped his left knee up on the bed, trailing my shoulder slowly "I met her a few years ago at an event. By then I had confirmed that I was bisexual but wasn't interested in anyone. She seemed sweet enough, from a wealthy background and approved by everyone so we started dating. It seemed normal and perfect, but within me I knew that wasn't what I wanted."

His finger traced down to my shoulder blade "When my dad signed all his shares to me I proposed to her. Lauren was over the moon and I remembered that moment when I slipped that ring on her finger. I felt happy and trapped at the same time."

I shivered in delight as his finger reached the small of my back "So a few days later I broke it off." My eyes widened "Are you serious?"

But the expression he was sporting told me that this was no joke "Her father threatened my dad, going on about how I had embarrassed his family name and that it was all over the papers. My dad took it reasonably; he wasn't even angry which made me feel worse. He told me that if I felt like something was weighing me down or made me feel unhappy that I shouldn't ever hesitate to get out."

Right now I definitely respected the older Mr. Gold right now.

Axel pressed a kiss on my shoulder "Lauren represented everything that people expected me to be but I couldn't. A young successful heir with a dashing socialite wife and what not, never mind that I wasn't happy. But when I met you-"

He paused his actions for a moment making my breath hitch "Not once did I hesitate. With Lauren it took constant nagging to get me to go out for dinner and events etc. but with you I never ever stopped to think about it. That morning when you told me your name I got a PI to search you."

I cast a questioning glance his way and he sent me a guilty one right back. "After knowing all I wanted about you I wanted to make you mine. I didn't care about the looks or doubts, all that made sense was me having you because never did I ever feel unsure about you."

Axel's confession had ripped the oxygen from my lungs and thrown it to some other distant planet. Seeing him this way made me feel happy, secure in my feelings. There were no words for me really top that so I kissed him slowly savouring the feel of his sinful lips. There was a moment of silence, comfortable silence. Without words he had understood exactly what I meant to say to him.

"We made some pretty good memories on this boat." I said after a while.

Axel shifted sitting upright smirking "Beats getting high on the deck." I groaned burying my face in his bicep "Don't remind me. That would be one of the worst decisions of my life, apart from the fact that I met you even though you scared the fuck outta me. What were you even doing here at 2 AM?"

"Sometimes I like to relax here away from everyone and all the stress. Even if it's for a few hours." He explained. I brushed my fingers on the strange bird tattoo with the words phoenix at the bottom in fancy writing on his shoulder. It enthralled me because it seemed like he had quite a thing for phoenixes.

"That's my mother's name." Axel stated quietly.

I shifted to face him "What?"

"Phoenix was my mother's name." he repeated.

"Oh." That was all I said. It was admirable in my eyes that he honoured his mother more than anyone else. Even if it was naming his boat after her or tattooing her name and symbol on his arm.

"That was my first tattoo. Got it when I was about 16, before my whole rebellious phase began." Axel leaned so he was staring directly at me. "You know she loved sailing? It was always her dream to sail somewhere far away but she never got the chance."

There was no mistaking the sadness in his voice.

"Will you tell me about her?" I asked softly.

"Someday yeah. But for now I just want you to stick around for me." His eyes shone with something along the lines of sincerity and vulnerability. "Right now I'm not ready for a lot of things but when I am I want you to be there with me ok? Just know that I care for you so fucking much and because of you I want to be ready."

His words made my eyes prickle with unshed tears. "I'll stay Axel." And I meant it completely. Axel kissed me hard and dirty the way I loved allowing me to thread my fingers in his hair. Then he sucked another mark into me neck like the possessive bastard he was.

"We should probably off now. We've been cooped up in here for a really long time." He said eyeing my plump and swollen lips.

I groaned "Do we have to?"

He grinned wickedly "I'm pretty sure Bill is tired of pretending he's not here. Plus I don't want anyone to think that I've kidnapped you."

I rolled my eyes fine. Axel stood up from the bed in all his naked glory leaving me to admire his firm muscles and luscious ink scattered skin. "There's a shower you know."

"And?"

"We could shower." He said picking up our clothes from the floor. I raised my eyebrow "Is that all we'd be doing?"

He shrugged innocently "And we could try to attempt some dirty feats while in the shower."

I grinned sitting up "We should probably go shower yeah."

Our boys are opening up! More happy feels to come don't worry!

Chapter 15 - Old Flames & New Habits

"I expect to get results by the end of today. I personally told you the importance of getting that merger done Gabriel." Axel's irritated voice woke me up from my deep slumber. I was sleeping in the master bedroom inhaling his familiar scent on the pillows. It was a mystery why the real thing wasn't here with me. I moved around the bed groaning at how cold Axel's side felt meaning that he hadn't been in bed for some time now.

He was probably in the living room taking one of his important business calls.

The blinking alarm beside me showed 6:43 meaning I would have to get out of bed in the next 20 minutes since I had a lecture at 9. Going to lectures weren't fun or anything but I was glad to go since it meant that stability was back in my life.

Doing nothing but recovering at home can make a guy slowly go nuts especially since Axel acts like I'm going to break skull every time I try to do stuff for myself. I'll admit that it's nice being pampered once in a while but I'm used to taking care of myself for so long.

"Yes Gabriel and make sure it's signed before any of the ships leave the port."

I shut my eyes for a few more minutes before dragging my tired body from the warm king-sized bed. I used to think it's so cliché for rich people to like huge beds but after sleeping on the 1000 count threadbare Egyptian cotton, I can definitely see the appeal.

I stripped away my pyjamas and turned on the shower, waiting a few minutes before I got in. Unlike most people I prefer to take cold showers in the morning to wake me up properly. Not to mention that it makes me feel a lot better than warm showers sometimes. After fifteen minutes I finished, wearing my boxers and the loose fitting T-shirt that I wore to sleep.

Axel was still on the phone when I went to the living room. He was wearing nothing but a pair of low riding dark blue basketball shorts and black Nikes. His chest was bare and glistening with sweat meaning that he had just come from the gym. If my brain wasn't half asleep the sight alone would have been enough for my boxers to drop instantly.

It was obvious that the caller was not making him very happy by his expression but on noticing my presence it softened up "Just do it by the end of today Gabriel." He dropped the line.

"Hey good morning." Axel greeted pecking me lightly on the lips.

"Morning, you weren't in bed." I mumbled against his lips. He kissed me some more "Sorry love had to do some work and decided to hit the gym."

"I want to hold you, but you're all sweaty now." I whined placing my arms safely around his shoulders. His laughter was rich and hearty "Just hug me it's no big deal."

"Not when I just showered." I said trying to make him see my dilemma.

He peppered kisses on my neck "No problem, you can always shower with me again." The innuendo was obvious "And again."

"As much as I want to do that, I really have to get ready to go to class. Finals are almost here." I stated not wanting to give in just yet.

Axel sighed "Fine. Guess I couldn't keep you locked up as my special prisoner forever."

I giggled "Don't worry. Tonight I'll let you imprison me anyhow you want." He groaned at the thought kissing me even harder than before.

We made out for some time before I managed to drag myself away to the kitchen to make us both breakfast while he showered alone. By the time I was done with it Axel had appeared barefoot and shirtless with his hair still in wet spikes. He looked like he was ready for a lazy day at home.

"Aren't you going to work today?" I asked curiously setting the plate of waffles on the breakfast bar in front of him. There was a dining table with nice white cushion chairs but I didn't see the need for it since we always ate at the breakfast bar. It felt less formal that way.

"Yes but much later." He explained taking a bite. Hmm, perks of being the boss I guess.

I shrugged sitting beside him on the glass dining table. The situation felt oddly domestic, something I was getting used to while staying with Axel these past few days. It was different, but felt good. Anyone would feel good if it meant waking up next to their object of affection every morning. Axel was paying an awful amount of attention to his phone the table with a scowl on his face as if the contents of whatever he was reading had annoyed him in someway.

"Timothy's driving you to the campus." He stated.

I looked up in confusion "What? But I can take the bus like I always do." Why would he need Timothy to drive me?

"Kendall two men tried to kidnap you almost a week ago. By sheer luck they didn't succeed." Axel said matter-of-factly. "I'll feel much better if you're in secure hands."

"They're in prison now." I tried to reason.

He dropped his fork "But nobody knows if they were working alone or if someone sent them. Love your safety is more important to me right now so no more questions. End of discussion."

My mouth was wide open. Seeing him make decisions without consulting me made me feel like some handicapped schoolchild. I understood the situation from his point of view but he could have at least told me something beforehand. And yet he had to audacity to go all 'end of discussion' with me.

"It's for your own good." Axel said in a softer tone.

"I know but I don't like you making decisions without telling me first. You didn't even bring this up last night so I'd be prepared mentally." I answered playing with my fork. I'm not exactly cheerleading to the idea that my boyfriend has to drive me everywhere, even if it sort of for safety reasons.

"Are you mad at me?"

Of course not! Well somewhat irritated could be the word since I prefer to be told things beforehand. But I wasn't angry with him, so far from it.

"I'm not mad at you." I explained holding his hand. "I just wish you told me sooner. You can't exactly make plans without bringing me on board first. That way I feel as though my opinions are valid."

"Ok." He looked relived "My mind just keeps playing back to when I saw you in the hospital. That's a position I never want you to be in again." Gosh this man melted me in ways I didn't even know were possible.

"Your opinions are relevant to me Kendall. But when it comes to your safety don't be surprised if I make any decisions based on what I think is best for you." he explained.

In his own over-bearing way this Axel being caring so I probably shouldn't give him too much hell.

I smiled "I understand." I kissed him chastely on the lips. Axel whispered to my lips "I'm glad you're not mad at me."

He could make the ground rumble with that earth-shattering aura of his, but still managed to act like a bleak little lamb around me sometimes.

There was a light pat on my ass "Now go dress up before you make me forget all about my breakfast." I rolled my eyes hopping off the stool to go to the master bedroom. As soon as I was done I went back to the kitchen to see him still scrolling on his phone.

"Am I taking the town car?" I asked nervously.

"Of course not. Timothy will drive you with one of the SUV's." He replied. Even though I wasn't very happy with his choice, I'm glad we weren't taking the town car and attracting more attention than usual.

"Great I'll see you later." I said stuffing my laptop and other notes into my messenger bag.

"I might be late tonight but not so much." Axel stood up from the stool coming over to meet me.

"I'll wait up." I assured him kissing those addictive lips that I loved so much. His arms went around my waist pulling me closer to his body. His

Old Spice body wash wafted through my nostrils making me want to bury my head in his neck forever. But there was a very inconveniencing early morning lecture waiting for me which I would surely miss if I didn't start going now.

"Axel I have to go now." I mumbled.

"I know." He replied without moving an inch. I sighed "You can seduce me later please."

"You make me sound like some old horny bastard when you say that." He complained making me laugh.

"But you are old and horny." I teased making his grip on me firmer.

"Well you're a minx who smiles like an angel but can screw like a possessed demon but you don't see me using that against you." There was no describing how red that statement made my face.

"But I won't keep you any longer now. Stay out of trouble and I'll see you later." He breathed out kissing me one last time "Timothy's waiting for you downstairs."

I nodded picking up my messenger bag "Alright thanks. See you tonight so don't get too bored without me."

"Oh I'll be here working and wanking to thoughts of you like the perverted old man I am." He said dryly.

I rolled my eyes smiling fondly I got into the elevator. Hans the middle-aged doorman greeted me with a smile as while I strolled out of the building. He was pretty cool and didn't look at me weirdly unlike almost everyone else in here.

True enough, Timothy was waiting in front with the black Range Rover vogue.

"Good morning Mr. Ross." He greeted.

"Hi Timothy." I squeaked. Don't blame me too much seeing as this is the first time he's actually talked to me alone.

"Are we heading to the university now?" he asked once I was seated in the back.

"Yes."

The drive was silent and I kept playing with my fingers all through. And to think I thought high school would be the last time I would need a pick and drop. The truth was that I was much more worried about descending from such a fancy ride. Sure everyone assumed that college is supposed to be the time when appearances don't matter but people still gossiped.

There might not bullies who physically shove you into lockers anymore, but words and rumours still thrive bountifully.

We arrived but I told Timothy to park a little further from where I usually drop off. He was about to open the door for me but I politely declined. I won't be surprised if Axel put him up to that.

"Should I pick you around five?" Timothy asked.

"Yes that's fine and at this same spot if you don't mind. Thank you." I replied since I was meaning to go to the library. He nodded driving away.

Despite how careful I thought I was being, I noticed that some people eyed me curiously, obviously wondering when I changed my means of transportation. I wasn't popular or well known in anyway but I guess even the smallest changes are noticed by some people.

My first lecture droned on pretty quickly, which I was grateful for. Pierce texted me sometime around noon but he wasn't free yet so we couldn't meet up any time soon. Even though I enjoyed staying with Axel I still missed my roommate very much. He had told me when I called him that enjoyed having the place all to himself (but I knew that was code for he was lonely and hated watching How To Get Away With Murder alone).

"Kendall." Someone interrupted my thinking.

"Oh hi James." I greeted as he sat on the chair next to me in the library. "What's up?" Our last meeting was tension filled but I hoped we would still be able talk out like friends.

"Pierce told me you were in the hospital for a while. How are you feeling now?" He sounded worried.

I smiled "Thanks for your concern but I'm fine now."

"I dropped by to see you but Pierce told me you weren't staying at your apartment for some time. Did you move out or something?"

I curled my lip knowing where this was going already "Yeah I'm uh staying somewhere else for now."

"Where?" James asked obviously curious as to how I moved so quickly.

"I haven't moved or anything yet. I'm staying with my boyfriend for a little while." I said playing with pen. The news obviously surprised him because his mouth hung open for a moment before he closed it.

"Oh." James tried to remain composed "That's great for you I guess. I was just under the impression that you were still single."

"It's not been going on for long." I explained "We just recently got into it. But we've been seeing each other a little while."

"Is it that guy you were with last time?" is it me or did James sound kind of hardened? I nodded slowly "Uh yeah? Is anything wrong?"

"No." He said coldly. "I should probably go now. Don't wanna keep you from your work." And with that he stood up without letting me say a single word after. What was his problem all of a sudden? James was never really close to me in the first place but lately he's been acting like I've betrayed his trust or something.

It's annoying and confusing at the same time.

Honestly I don't need the people around me making my life more complicated. I'm still figuring this whole assault issue and Mara even if she's gone, is still winding up screws in my head because my sister is the most troublesome person I know. She may have come with the whole intention of scaring me, but I know that's not her only reason which frightened me even more.

The only thing that seems somewhat calming is Axel. Sure we're still getting to understand each other more than ever, but a part of me feels like I've known him forever. There are still a lot of thing I've yet to tell him, but for now I'm going to bask in the steady pace we've set for now.

My phone buzzed meaning I got a text. I checked and fluttered internally when it said Axel.

Thinking about you in the midst of boring meetings ;)

I snorted replying him

You shouldn't text me during meetings. I don't think the boss would like that

He replied a minute later.

But I am the boss and I like texting my sexy little boyfriend

Ah that title made me blush internally. All other wandering thoughts of James evaporated instantly.

I'd like to talk to you more but I've got a two volume textbook to study Mr. CEO

His reply came in a lot later.

I got you a little present earlier but you'll see it when you get home

A present? He didn't tell me anything about a present before I left. I prayed that it wasn't some impulse buy or another watch.

What is it?

When you get home babe xxx

Wow those x's at the end made me laugh out due to our running joke of him being an old man. Axel was in no way old but our age difference was the cause of it all.

Five pm rolled around pretty quickly and in no time Timothy was waiting for me at the spot he dropped me off. It made me wonder what he did during the day and how the hell he mastered the art of getting here on time.

"Good evening Mr. Ross." He greeted.

"Kendall's just fine with me." I smiled entering the car. He raised an eyebrow "Mr. Ross is what I've been asked to address you by."

Ok then. I nodded as he drove off back the penthouse still wondering what Axel had gotten for me in such a short time. In any case I would be patient and see it before deciding if he had been rational or not.

"Goodnight Mr. Ross." Timothy said as we stopped in front of the building.

"Goodnight Timothy."

All I was thinking about now was going upstairs and taking a super long shower and maybe jumping Axel when he came back home if I still had any strength inside me. But the sight I met on coming back was not what I expected at all.

Seated on the dining table was a beautiful caramel skinned woman wearing a sleeveless white jumper and 6 inch heels scrolling frantically on her iPad. There was a designer handbag on the breakfast bar with matching luggage with the initials SB engraved on it.

"How did you get in here?" I asked startling her.

She stared at me puzzled "Who are you?" her accent wasn't British. It was something on the lines of French and American.

"Um I'm the boyfriend of the guy who owns this apartment." I replied wondering if this was a god time to alert security or not.

She palmed her forehead "That idiot's done it again. He never tells me anything anymore."

What the hell was she talking about?

Don't worry, Axel isn't in that much trouble.......yet. Vote + Comment and consider this update my early present to you all ;)

Chapter 16 - Honest Intentions

"Um I don't mean to sound rude, but what the hell are you doing here?" I asked the seemingly distraught woman in front of me.

She groaned "I'm going to kill Axel. Like murder. Like tear him limb from limb while watch the life gradually leave his body."

What?

I wasn't sure if she was joking or not so I casually eyed the kitchen counter for anything that could be used as a weapon. "You are joking right?" I asked nervously.

She sighed "On a scale from one to ten, I'm as serious as a twenty." Shit! This mysterious woman who I knew nothing about was really starting to scare me, on serious level now. I wondered how she managed to get in since the security here is probably worse than Fort Knox. The only way I get in is because my name is on Axel's personal guest list. So that means-

"Kendall?" Axel called out from the front door. I immediately flailed to his side trying to warn him "Axel no there's a crazy woman-"

"What?" he looked obviously dumbstruck. Suddenly the woman emerged looking pissed as ever "Axel you stupid fucker!" before anyone could do anything to stop her, the large designer handbag landed with a thud on his head.

"Ow! Shorty?! You're back already?" He sounded confused in the mist of his pain. She glared at him "Don't you Shorty me! I'm only gone for a little while and you fail to tell me that you're in a relationship? I had to hear it from Martin!"

He grunted rubbing his head "Of course he told you."

She folded her hands across her chest "Three months I was gone and you never mentioned once about anything interesting going on in your personal life."

"I'm sorry-"

She raised a hand "Save it. The only way my forgiveness can be bought if you buy me this new Hermes scarf I've been eyeing and promise to never leave me out of something in your life."

"Done." He replied with hesitating.

"Now give me a hug." She commanded but in a soft tone. Axel smiled slightly giving her a full body hug "I missed you Shorty."

"And I've missed you a lot Axel. My life isn't the same unless I'm constantly reprimanding you for some stupid mistake you've made."

He rolled his eyes pulling away "What meaning does my life have without you?"

I stared at both of them "I'm obviously missing something so do you mind telling me what's going on?"

Axel turned to me "Sorry love this is Shorty Blue my childhood friend." He referred to her with a certain fondness that one couldn't mistake for anything more than a sacred friendship. "And Shorty this is my boyfriend Kendall."

Shorty smiled at me "Are you legal?"

I blinked looking baffled "Um yeah."

"Good." Then she hugged me. It felt kind of awkward at first but something within me advised me to let go. "Sorry, sometimes I don't trust Axel when his pants are involved."

"Is Shorty Blue really your name?" I asked. But instead of her getting offended as I expected, she laughed tipping her head back and I realized that she was one of those people who could swim in cheese and still manage to look perfect. Flawlessness came naturally to her.

"No darling it isn't. It's Chantelle Bloom but that doesn't sound so fun does it?" She asked. She was.....eccentric. That's an easy adjective.

"It's definitely fun." I replied.

She glanced at Axel "You've been keeping this lovely creature from me?"

"For a good reason." He murmured.

I beamed "Nice to meet you Shorty. I'm sorry that Axel didn't mention anything about you before."

Shorty sighed rather dramatically "He needs to accept that I'll always be around to interfere in his business. Anyway it was quite lovely meeting you Kendall but I'll be moving to my hotel now."

"You too." I mustered as politely as possible.

"I'll be back, preferably to interrogate you further." She stated casually picking up her purse from the counter along with her luggage. "End point, never try to hide stuff from me again Axel."

Honestly even I had to shiver at her tone. This was probably the only person who seemed to scare him and I've met Timothy before.

Axel pecked her on the cheek as her threat didn't faze him "It was lovely seeing you again."

"Likewise." She replied before leaving the penthouse while taking a gust of my sanity and oxygen along with her.

I faced my boyfriend "Can I ask what just happened, again?"

Axel laughed pouring himself some scotch. I had tried it a few days prior and declared it was the nastiest thing ever, perplexed as to why he guzzled it like water. "Something isn't she? Shorty is one of my only friends. We meet when we were teenagers and she had transferred here from France, right when she gave herself that nickname."

"She's quite something." I commented sitting on the snowy white couch.

He nodded loosened his tie "Shorty isn't the most law-abiding citizen on the planet, but her heart is rather warm. A good person."

I smirked placing my feet on the coffee table "Yeah she does kind of scare you."

Axel rolled his eyes "She's got this horrible maternal instinct with her, like she feels the need to check and beat to line if I'm misbehaving. Anyway she was in Jamaica for the time being on an in-prompt holiday but I guess she's back now."

I stood up from the couch "Her name was on your private visitor's list right?"

"Yes." He replied looking curious. I shrugged "No reason."

In the short span of time I'd know her, it didn't seem impossible for her to break in. Ok maybe that sounded a little judgmental. But still.

"I'm hungry. We should probably order pizza or something." I suggested moving to the fridge to get a drink. Axel drained the rest of his scotch "I brought your surprise with me."

"Oh." I had forgotten all about the texts and my worked up state when I met Shorty at the apartment. "What is it?" I asked going back to the couch with a Sprite in hand. He brought a blue box from his suit "Here."

"Ok." I dragged slowly wondering why my heart was beating so fast. I opened it gasped at the loveliest pair of cufflinks I had ever seen. No really, these were top notch stuff. Gold plated tips with a triskele design I had read about somewhere. It was the kind that if I had a million dollars to my name that I'd buy without hesitation.

"Axel I can't possibly accept this." I started still staring at them.

"Why not?" He sounded stiff.

I closed the box "Don't get me wrong I love it but you can't get me something as expensive as this, it's insane. I feel like I'm taking advantage of you."

"Look here." He made me face him by gently pushing my chin up "You're not taking advantage of me in anyway. I chose to buy them for you and I'll buy a thousand more if I have to. Giving you gifts is a way for me to say how much I care about you, don't even give me that bullshit about spending too much on you because I'll spend a million fucking pounds if I bloody feel like it, as long as it's on you."

His little speech made me smile a bit. "Fine but don't go overboard ok?"

"I'll go overboard if I fucking want to." He said a little stubbornly making me roll my eyes fondly as I pecked his lips.

"Besides this is also my way of asking you to go to my father's charity ball with me the night after tomorrow." Axel murmured to my lips.

"Your dad?" I said with my words slightly muffled due to his lips on mine.

"Hmm, he holds it every year for his organization which supports recovering drug addicts. It's called Warm Hands." He explained while bruising a mark into my neck at the same time.

Remarkable multitasking if you ask me.

I supressed a moan "That's pretty noble of him." It did sound like a worthy cause to me.

He stilled for a second "If you say so." Meeting the older Mr. Gold made me feel a bit weary though since I didn't know him and wasn't sure about his reaction when he finds out that his son is dating a male ten years younger than him.

"Don't overthink Kendall." He scolded biting down on my earlobe with his incisor making me let out a moan. "It'll be fine and I really do want you to meet my father." The statement made me squeal internally that he wanted me to meet his father.

I grabbed his face kissing him properly before pulling away "But please don't make a habit of buying me stuff whenever you want to ask me to go somewhere."

Axel frowned "Isn't it almost everyone's dream to have a dashing rich boyfriend who buys you stuff without you asking?"

That's the stereotype isn't it? "Well you're out of luck because I like you for your good looks and big cock not your money." I said feigning all seriousness.

He had an amused expression "So you'd want me even if I wasn't wealthy as long as my cock and face remain the same?"

I acted like I was thinking about it "Pretty much sums it."

"That does it. I'm gonna make you ride me so hard right here babe." He said practically tearing off his belt and pants. To that order I happily complied.

******

The next morning I woke up naked and sated under the sheets to the sight of Axel dressing up in one of his immaculate suits. The hot sex from last night had somehow rendered me in temporary paralysis so I just laid there watching him creepily. I'll admit that as much as I loved the bad boy look Axel sported with his casual attire, there was nothing more attractive than seeing him in his powerful designer suits looking like he was ready to take on the world.

"Some people consider staring to be disturbing."

I snorted "Well other people consider it to be a sign of admiration."

He took a paused from knotting his tie "Right now the one who should be admired is you."

"Because being naked with dried cum all over me and bed hair is a qualification for the world's sexiest." I deadpanned.

Axel sat down on the bed and stroked my cheek with his thumb "You're beautiful Kendall. Don't ever doubt that."

I nodded feeling my cheeks burn because of his compliment. He kissed my forehead "I'll see you later. Do you have any lectures today?" I shook my head "Then I'll see you tonight."

"Ok." I replied in a small voice. "Early morning meeting?" in regards to the time.

He sighed "Unfortunately. Stay safe love." And with that he left me alone in the penthouse to sleep since it was still pretty early. I considered calling Pierce if he wanted to hang out since I knew that he didn't have any lecture today, but his voicemail answered me instead and he shot me a text saying he was hanging out with a friend when I came out of the shower.

Huh weird.

I planned on just lazing around watching re-runs of episodes I missed during the week and maybe getting even farther ahead of my academics again. But my plans were thwarted as soon as I got a call from the lobby saying that a Miss. Shorty Blue wanted to come up to the apartment to see me. Dazzled I told them to let her up.

She waltzed from the elevator "Get dressed we're going out."

No good morning, no how are you. Just an intimidating gaze which froze me and the cup of coffee in my hand. "Um, where?"

Shorty raised an eyebrow "Oh that's right I forgot. Axel was in a meeting this morning but he told me to take you out shopping."

"He did? But this morning he didn't say anything to me." I said.

"He called me hastily a while ago like it was something he remembered last minute." She explained.

"Ok." I said slowly.

Shorty placed her hands on the waist barely ruffling her silk top "And why are you still standing there?"

That made me scramble down to the main bedroom in record time to change out of my pyjamas. When I emerged Shorty looked distastefully at my outfit which consisted of skinny jeans, my DC shirt and Supras. She wasn't even saying much yet I cowered under her gaze. Leave it to Axel to befriend a scary fashionista.

"Thank heavens we're going shopping pronto." She exclaimed. It was probably an allergic reaction to anything that wasn't Chanel or Gucci. Not that I blamed her for it.

"I don't really have much clothes over here." I said awkwardly.

She sighed placing her manicured hands on her forehead "Alright let's just go." I followed her to the elevator enduring the two minutes of awkward silence until we got to the lobby where I tried to keep up with her pace. She was pretty fast for a woman in 6 inch Louboutins.

"Goodbye Hans." She said with more vigour meaning she probably knew him well.

My mouth dropped to the ground when I saw her ride.

"That's your car?!"

"Yes." She answered with hidden smug. But she had every right to sound smug with that wicked looking silver Maserati in front of us "Holy fuck, this just came out and it costs like $150, 000."

"Well you can gawk from inside." Shorty said breezily hopping in while I rushed to the passenger seat all but giddy.

Pierce would be so jealous since he's a car freak.

She started the car and swerved on the street like a pro. It was when she got to the main road that she pushed down her designer glasses perched from their position perched on top of her head to interrogate me.

"Now I'm only going to ask this once; what are your intentions with Axel?"

"Isn't that supposed to be the other way around?" I asked but her expression was sharp making me gulp.

"I'm serious Kendall." Her tone alone told me that. "Axel is like a - scratch that, he is my brother. And even when he has his head so far stuck up his ass I will continue to look out for him till the day I die. Now I don't have to tell you how serious that commitment is so if you're planning on screwing up Axel's life, you better walk out of his life now because when that day comes I'll unleash revenge so bad that even deities will marvel at."

I nodded; I was both impressed and terrified "Look, I don't have to give you some rivalling speech to make. But I want you to know that I care for him a lot."

Her lips curled "How much?"

"Too much." I replied honestly. "I've never really been serious with anybody but him in my life. Part of me worries that I'm not good enough for him due to my age and experience, but I'm still surprised that he wants to be with me. I admire your devotion to him and I also want to let you know that if I ever screw up I'll be the one to seek you out first. Because I-"

My breathing hitched "I care about him that much." I felt heavy because I meant every single word I said.

Shorty was silent for a while. We stopped at a traffic light "Is it that you're that good of an actor or you're really telling the truth?"

"What do you think?" I asked staring at me fingers.

For the first time a genuine smile fitted her lips "I'm thinking of whooping Axel's behind for not telling me about you sooner."

I grinned "Not too hard though. I still need it."

"Right." She replied.

"You guys have been friends for a really long while."

"Yes since high school. Back then he was the sweet adorable Econ dork, not this big shot everyone over respects." I smiled thinking about Axel as a nerd.

"But you don't have an English accent?"

Shorty snorted "Well I don't fancy sounding like I've got carrots up my nose thank you." the only accent I've ever really liked is Axel's. "Besides I'm French Canadian actually so I spend my time abroad more than here."

I thought she was American actually.

We arrived at Burberry's not long after. "Really?"

Shorty gave a cross look "Where did you think Levi's?" with an actual shudder as she left the car. I trailed after her wondering if it's possible to feel underdressed while going shopping. The entire store felt like it was going to spit me out because of how out of place I felt.

A short pudgy woman in a blue appeared "Chantelle!"

"Hilda!"

They did the rich people kissing thing on the cheek "You've been gone an awfully long time. We've got some new coats and bags that just came in." she whispers like it's a secret.

Shorty looked equally enthralled "That sounds lovely but I'm not here for me."

Both women gazed at me while I just stood awkwardly.

"And he is.....?"

"My new boy toy. I'm trying do him up for this event I'm going to tomorrow but he's a little underdone so you'll have to start basic." Shorty said making me gawk at her in surprise. Boy toy?!

Hilda looked at me with a sort of judgemental glare "I'll see what I can do."

"Really? Boy toy?" I asked once Hilda had left.

"Sweetheart until you've been plucked thoroughly there's no way I'm introducing you as Axel's boyfriend. You're not on that level yet." She replied.

I cocked an eyebrow "So I'm at you're level?"

She smirked "Oh darling, just being in my shadow alone is enough to make you look good."

Ok I deserve an award for writing that chapter will a full tummy and spliting headache. Anyways hope you'll loved it because i suffered for it ;) Lol.

How do you guys like Shorty Blue? Believe or not she's based on someone I know *shudders* but in a good way. Next update comes with a special announcement but for now, Happy Holidays to those who celebrate Christmas.

xx

Chapter 17- Posh & Becks Part 1

You guys will not believe the massive writer's block I fought while writing this. In fact I was going to update a lot later, but I didn't want to disappoint all you lovely people. Anyways my grandparents sent me a fancy espresso machine for Chrismas since I love coffee so much but I'm still trying to figure it and I'm frustrated and caffine depreived.

This is going to be long so I did it in a part 1 & 2 again. Anyways, enjoy while I keep on screaming at this bloodly thing :)

Needless to say, by the time we were I'm sure that the amount of clothes we acquired was worth my tuition for the year even though I wasn't allowed to view the price tags. I was fairly certain that I only needed one outfit but Shorty glared when I reminded her and I ended up with up to a dozen outfits.

In fact I'm pretty sure I wasn't hallucinating when I noticed Axel's silver credit card smoke a bit when it was swiped from the amount of money spent. It made me cringe even more than necessary.

"We would have hit some more stores but I have somewhere else to be." Shorty said in a truly disappointed tone as the bags were shoved into the car.

"I'm sure this is enough." I said not wanting to upset her. I'm no psychologist but I'm pretty sure she must have been deprived of a playmate when she was a child because she took delight in dressing me up like her own personal Ken doll until I had to beg her to stop in fear of the dent in Axel's bank account. Sure I knew he could afford it but that gave me no right to be inconsiderate.

Plus I was raised in a family where if it costs more than $20 it is heart-depleting. Just joking but you catch my drift.

"Are you coming to the charity gala?" I asked.

"Of course. We've been going for a long time. Axel's father is one of my family's closet friends." Shorty replied keeping her eyes on the road. Again was the small slip in which no one mentioned his mother. I wondered what happened to her and why it had obviously affected Axel the way it did. I'm not nosy so I'm not going to try and pry into his business, but that little thread of curiosity will always be there.

*****

"For the record, you're not mad right?" I asked my boyfriend nervously. He smiled arranging his bow tie "For the last time Kendall, I'm not mad at you. And I assure you that my bank account is barely scratched."

"Are you sure?" My eyes widened.

I got a glance at the receipt when Shorty dropped me off and let's say it was a surprise that I didn't have a seizure right there on the sidewalk.

"Yes I am."

"Because if you had to file for bankruptcy I would feel really bad and-"

"Damn please give it a rest already. I told you that you were fairly under the limit so don't worry." Axel cut me off.

I curled my lip "Fairly?"

Suddenly his lips were pressed on mine to silence me. We kissed for about a few seconds before he pulled away raising an eyebrow as if to challenge me to ramble any further.

"Right, shutting up." I made a zipping motion.

He rolled his eyes fondly still adjusting his bow tie. At the moment we were in the back of the car driving to charity gala and my emotions were a mixture of excitement and nervousness. Although being with Axel had brought me into the light of finer living, tonight was the first time that I would actually see experience it first-hand. The world of the elites where I'm sure he blended in effortlessly.

And gosh I was shaking.

"For the record, you look hot." I commented trying to ease my nerves. Axel smiled "Thank you. Now please take a deep breath because I can practically hear your beating heart."

I took a mighty one "I'm sorry, just feeling anxious."

He kissed my knuckles "   It's no big deal. We will just hang around long enough for the auction and socialize with a few people I promise."

"Auction?" I questioned.

"There's always an auction where we get the money to donate to charity." He explained.

"What do they auction off?" I asked further.

He shrugged "Could be anything."

"Like?"

"I don't know." He obviously didn't feel like answering.

"Ok." I murmured. The car we were using today was a Bentley and that fact that I didn't swoon the way I'd normally do was enough proof that the evening jitters were really getting to me. I honestly didn't know why I was so nervous really. It was a party, no big deal. I had gone to Martin's art exhibit in the past, so why I was nearly tearing out my hair this time?

Probably because the situation was different then. Axel and I hadn't really defined our relationship outside the borders of great sex and occasional companionship.

But now we were a lot more serious. And that meant a lot more expectations and maybe people to please.

"I knew these cufflinks would look great on you." he admired brushing it with his thumb.

I was wearing a tux seeing as the occasion was far too formal for me to just pull off the blazer and jeans look I preferred. I wasn't a fan of suits but there was no denying that this one fitted me immensely exposing very little flaws and made me look a lot older.

"They're pretty nifty." I stated enjoying the way he massaged my wrist.

Axel kissed my knuckles "Everything looks flawless on you." that made my cheeks a little redder and my pants a little tighter but I was not going to get carried away at the back of the Bentley since it didn't have a partition like the town car. Although I doubt Timothy would act surprised.

Sometimes I'm sure a fly would perch on his face and the man wouldn't even notice due to his statue-like persona. The only time he reacts is when

Axel speaks to him or tells him to do something. It seemed impossible for any human to act this stoic.

"Is this the place?" I asked trying to hide the awe in my voice as we slowly parked in front of a massive house. I'd say mansion, but it didn't strike me as one of those large lifeless structures which only existed for show. In front was a massive fountain of a nymph with water pouring out of her open palm and a rose bush around it. In fact everything seemed to be covered by roses from what I saw, giving a sickly sweet feeling to any visitor coming in. There were massive white columns supporting the front but wrapped with vines quite impressively.

But all together it gave me a somewhat….welcome vibe. Like it wasn't just a house built for show but appeared to feel genuinely like a home.

The architect who designed this place did a superb job. I was so stuck on it that I didn't even notice Axel coming out of the car already.

"Welcome to my childhood home Kendall." He announced helping me out of the car.

"No words." I said still gazing "No words can describe how awesome this place is."

He chuckled "It's not all that great love."

I huffed "That's just something rich people say to sound modest. Well newsflash, this ain't modest in anyway."

Even without looking I could sense him rolling his eyes as he led us to the front door where a man I assumed was the butler was waiting as soon as we entered.

"Good evening Mr. Gold." He greeted.

"Evening Baxter." Axel replied smoothly keeping his hold on my arm. Soon enough we were surrounded by many other men and women all dressed like royalty. I didn't expect anything less seeing as Fletcher Shipping wasn't just a small business. I learned a while ago that they were the 2nd biggest shipping magnate in the UK courtesy of Google since I knew Axel would never tell me that voluntary.

The interior was just as impressive with more than six chandeliers lighting the room and classic but tasteful decorating. There were several antique paintings which made me guess that the older Mr. Gold was an art appreciator in the true sense. I was really impressed.

A waiter appeared offering champagne which I gladly accepted guzzling it down in an effort to reduce my still very-present nerves. Several guests came to meet Axel congratulating him on the success his company had made or telling him how wonderful his father was.

I just stayed still at his side with a stiff smile and politely answering the one or two questions thrown my way probably in an effort not to appear rude. Axel conversed and questioned with all the finesse his possessed adding another feature to the reasons why I admired this man. His way with words so silky and smooth, showing not a speck of doubt or hesitance and answering with all the renowned confidence in the world.

His hand firmly placed on the small of my back like it was the most natural thing in the world making me feel a lot bolder. We didn't get as much stares as I thought we would, as if the people really didn't mind that I was a man. But it would be foolish to think that everyone was fine with it.

However I was happy that those who weren't didn't show it.

"Tom, wonderful to see you." He said shaking an attractive man wearing a pristine white tuxedo.

"Ah Axel Gold always a pleasure." Tom replied sounding a lot more genuine than most of the other guests before letting his eyes fall on me. "I don't think I've met your friend before."

"No you haven't. Tom this is Kendall Ross my date. Kendall, meet Tom Niles a brilliant banker but a very lousy poker player." He smirked.

The man laughed heartily "Of course we can't be lucky with numbers always. To be honest I'm surprised that you keep up with this bloke at all. I've always thought him to be the monk type."

"Well you thought wrong." Axel replied a little too sweetly.

"I handle him just fine since he doesn't misbehave around me too much." I said with a side smile.

Tom eyed me curiously "American aren't you?"

I affirmed so. He nodded "A wonderful country even if they're so bloody confused most of the time. It's the democrat and republican debates that I enjoy the most. Now if I was American I'd be a republican. Probably among those who were anti-welfare, but still republican."

I raised an eyebrow "Well then, wouldn't you like to know what kind of republican I am?"

He looked surprised for a moment before bursting into laughter "You've gotten yourself a smart one Axel my boy."

Axel's hold on my waist grew firmer but not uncomfortable "I sure have." Tom excused himself to see another business partner who had arrived.

"And here I was thinking that you're only smart-mouthed with me." He said with his lips twitching. I sipped my champagne trying to look innocent "I can't have him doubting my nationality can I?"

He whispered something along the lines of "little minx" behind my ear before I saw a familiar face and grinned.

"Martin!"

The blonde gave me a full hug "Great to see you again Kendall." He was bursting with energy as always but this time wearing a black cut blazer and a shirt with matching shoes. This was the only time I'd ever seen him without some sort of head wear but of course he'd pull off another outrageous outfit and look great in it.

"Are you girlfriends done kissing up?" Axel teased and Martin flipped him off.

"Spencer's near the band with the other old men." He retorted with a smirk making me laugh a little. Axel only pretended to act offended but gave him a brotherly pat and kissed my forehead before going to talk "business" with Spencer.

"I'm glad you're much better. Didn't particularly like seeing you hooked up in the hospital like that."

"Me either." My eyes darted to where Axel was talking seriously with Spencer about something.

"I'm glad you two are back together." He commented obviously knowing who I was just staring at.

"Yeah I'm glad too." I replied sipping my champagne.

"So how've you been faring all night?" Martin asked shoving his right hand into his pocket. I shrugged "A little nervous but I'm kind of over it. I was worried that I'd do something embarrassing in front of all these people."

He nodded "This is kind of my second drink. Been avoiding some people tonight."

"Like how?" I failed at keeping away the curiosity in my voice.

"My parents." He said emotionlessly. "They always come every year and this year is really no different. I don't need them reminding me how I'm throwing my life away for such a useless profession as art."

His tone was slightly bitter and pinched at my heart. "Sorry about dude. At least you're great at what you do."

Martin snorted "They don't care. As long as I'm not some high powered lawyer they'll never be proud. Although it's funny that the same lawyer they kept comparing me with is who I fell in love with."

Wow, now that is a twist.

"That's crazy." I couldn't help but say making him smile a lot more.

"Yeah it is. We met during some boring party and my dad introduced us after hearing that his dad owned one of the best law firms in England with like a 92% success rate." The fuck?! That's pretty high.

He had this wistful look in his eye "My dad thought that Spencer would give up a good front and convince me to become a lawyer. Too bad he convinced me in another direction."

I couldn't help but grin at his words. It made me pretty sad when parents try to mould their children into something they aren't. Don't get me wrong, I do believe parents should guide their children into making right choices. But not zombifying them into stuff that makes them unhappy.

Martin's lucky that he met the love of his life at the end of the day.

"Can you even imagine me as a lawyer?" he asked with an actual snort. "Spencer does pull off the whole badass attorney thing but I can't imagine myself arguing for a living. At least with art everything comes naturally to me."

"You'd be the first hipster lawyer." I suggested.

He giggled "Probably piss off the judge a lot."

We laughed together like actual girlfriends but I didn't really care since Martin was the only person apart from Axel and Pierce who I felt open with.

"You two cackling behind our backs?" Spencer appeared suddenly startling me but Martin practically jumped like a little puppy.

"Eh, maybe." I answered feeling a small peck on my cheek from Axel. "Nice to see you again Spencer."

"You two Kendall. Axel doesn't like bringing you out much." He eyed his best friend playfully.

"Well can you blame me?" Axel asked with exaggerated gusto.

Martin pouted "They're here babe."

Spencer frowned slightly at his boyfriend's discomfort "Let's go out back then. I really don't need your dad telling me how I've corrupted his young son. Again."

I had to stop myself from doing some ridiculous – like cooing when he placed his head cutely on Spencer's shoulder as they both walked away.

"They're both so in tune it's sickening." Axel commented on his friends with a fond expression.

"Yeah but in a good way."

He cocked an eyebrow "And I suppose you should explain to me how there's a good sickening?"

I rolled my eyes "Like you're so sickeningly hot you know?"

"I know." He replied arrogantly. His arms circled my waist "It's almost time for the auction darling, let's go."

Chapter 18- Posh & Beck Part 2

The auction took place in a large room with forest green walls. Waiters flanked around with their cloth-covered trays making sure that the guests were properly supplied with drinks at the times they were needed. If I didn't know any better I'd say that it was a ploy to get everyone drunk enough to bid more money. I might be wrong but who knows?

Axel led us to the seats somewhere in the middle where the view was still great but we didn't have to suffer none privacy offered in front.

"Are you auctioning?" I asked him in a hushed voice.

He gave me a half smile "We'll see."

The MC, a tall somewhat lanky man in a shiny grey suit appeared on the makeshift stage thanking everyone for attending and explaining the charities objectives and goals within a time span. I had to say that I was really impressed with it and thought it was a truly honourable cause Warm Hands was doing for those suffering from hard substances. I also learned from Axel that the name referred to the fact that when drug addicts were going through withdrawal, one of the symptoms was cold hands. Thereby helping them warmed a place in their hearts and hands.

"Ladies and Gentleman the first volunteer for this auction, please welcome Kristina Jenkins." A tall gorgeous woman in a black strapped dress appeared standing next to the MC.

"This lovely lady as you all know is an Olympic medallist, successful model and philanthropist. Anyone interested in a dance with this beauty? The bidding starts at £200."

"£300!" a man in a grey tailcoat sitting on the same row as us shouted.

"£350." Another gentleman in the back stated.

"£400!"

"£550." I could hardly hold in my surprise. That was a lot of money. "£600."

"£700."

"£700, anyone looking to outbid that?" nobody answered. "The bidding goes to the gentleman there."

The tailcoat man smiled smugly.

I leaned towards Axel "Is he really spending that much on a dance?"

His lips twitched which they only did whenever he was trying not to smile "Why not? It's for a good cause."

"Next we have Brenda Nu, a talented opera singer I'm sure many of you are familiar with." He said referring to the petite Asian woman in a long sparkly dress who just appeared. "A kiss from this Far East angel is worth the £150 we are starting the bidding from."

"£250!" a French man started.

"£400." A pudgy looking man in a tuxedo challenged him.

I was in daze throughout the rest of the auction. Several models, actresses and even a few other celebrities I knew were auctioned off for outrageous amounts. I'll admit that maybe I was a bit too fascinated by the process but could you blame me really. Imagine my surprise when Martin was ushered on stage with a shy smile introduced as a budding young artist.

His bidding had reached almost £5000 when a rigid lady Axel told me was a baroness won out. He was to spend a full day with her and judging from the woman's expression she was very pleased with that. Urgh I just hope she isn't a cougar or something because she was bound to get shut down hard.

At the end the older Mr. Gold himself came on stage making my heart flip backwards. He was pretty old, but in a learned and wise form not the sickly frail way. In fact I dare say that he aged quite gracefully.

His hair was a mixture of grey and black streaks combed backwards to perfection and his voice was steady and powerful as he spoke. Honestly I could see so much of Axel in this man that even without the introduction I would guess correctly.

Throughout his speech I noticed that Axel was a bit hard eyed but I refused to ask him about it. I had already questioned him enough times and didn't want to appear as I couldn't mind my own business for one minute.

The MC came and whispered something in his ear. He cleared his throat "It seems that thanks to your generous donations we have acquired £1,367,000 in total."

There was a cheerful round of applause from the audience and I found myself also clapping due to the staggering number stated.

"That was quite eventful." I stated once the auction was officially over and people were now migrating back to the large hall where the main party was situated.

Axel snaked his arm around my waist "You'll get used to it."

I raised an eyebrow "Well do you intend to drag to more events against my will?"

"It's not like I can find another sass-mouthed substitute with such a perky bum as yours." He subtly patted my ass smiling wickedly.

I gasped feigning horror "Flattery will get you absolutely everywhere." He winked dragging me closer to his side "Now there's someone I'd like you to meet."

"Who?"

"Hi dad." His greeted made me freeze for half a second before my brain finally processed that the figure standing before me was the older Mr. Gold in the flesh. Gosh he looked even more handsome and intimating up close.

"Meeting the Queen in the flesh seems more likely than running into you Axel. Can't even stop by to greet your old man." He joked spreading his arms open. Axel grinned to my surprise like a little boy eagerly hugging his father.

"Sorry about that dad." He apologized.

"The only person kind enough to keep me company tonight was Chantelle even though her talk about the traditional Caribbean naked weddings still has me in doubt." Mr. Gold stated like it was a fond but disturbing memory. I guess it as Shorty's all-round nature to spew disturbing stories.

"Work has been keeping me busy." He explained.

Mr. Gold nodded "You've been doing a wonderful job so far. I heard about the Fresny deal and I am absolutely impressed."

"Thanks dad." Axel sounded like his opinion truly meant the world. His attention turned to me and I tried not to cringe visibly. But he wasn't staring at me with disapproving or judgemental eyes. He looked at me curiously, like he was trying to decipher something really puzzling.

"Dad this is Kendall Ross my boyfriend, Kendall Ross this is my father." Axel introduced oblivious to my fear.

I swallowed stretching my hand for a shake "Nice to meet you Mr. Gold."

"Please, I reserve Mr. Gold for boardroom members I want to scare. Call me Theodore son." He replied shaking me with a friendly smile. I smiled back nearly pissing myself in relief. Ok he wasn't the typical homophobic prick I expected.

"Axel what stories about me have you told about me? The boy looks as white as a ghost." Theodore scolded.

Axel raised his hands in defeat "None I promise."

"I'm just really nervous about meeting a man as important as you sir." I tried to explain.

Theodore gave me a look "In all I am just a man. No need to look like you're about to get whipped. You look like Axel when he used to steal macaroons without his mother's permission."

"Dad." He groaned making the both of us laugh. I felt stupid for feeling so scared about meeting Mr. Go- Theodore. He seemed like a genuinely nice man who seemed to care more about his son's well-being and happiness more than the fact that he had a boyfriend.

"Well you haven't dated since you were sixteen so I'm going to make up for those years I didn't get to embarrass you in front of anyone." Theodore said matter-of-factly.

Axel rolled his eyes "Now you see why I moved out." It was surprising how he had turned into a pouty teenager after just a little while in his father's presence.

"Urgh, Nicolas Hale seems to have spotted me to nag about his merger. Be right back love." He squeezed my shoulder before going off.

"So you're a university student Kendall." Theodore turned his attention towards me.

I nodded "Yes sir. I'm studying English Literature but minoring in Political Science."

He hummed "Quite a lovely course. What are you hoping to become in future?"

"I'd probably work in a publishing company or write my own book to get published." I said. Theodore placed his hand on my shoulder "I hope my son is treating you properly. We both know he can be quite a handful."

I laughed "Yes sir he's been treating me right."

"It may seem surprising for most people but Axel being gay does not bother me one bit." He said as if he had read my mind throughout our entire conversation. "I'm just glad that he's found a companion in you."

"Me too sir." I replied.

He got a distant look "My son is the most important person in my life right now, ever since his mother passed away and she was his best friend." A deep pang went through my chest. No wonder he's always so touchy when it comes to her.

"You seem nice enough even if you are younger than him. I just want you to promise me that if you really care for him, don't leave him. I'm sure you're matured enough so I don't have to give you a list of threats for hurting Axel."

He hesitated for a moment "But something tells me that you might be right for him so please stay in his life."

"I promise sir." I said surprised by the fierce honesty in my own words.

Theodore gave me a friendly pat "A promise is debt my boy."

"What did I miss?" Axel appeared once again holding my waist which I've noticed must be his favourite thing to do.

"I've just been asking Kendall if you've been taking care of him properly."

He scoffed "You bet I have." Seriously, annoyed adolescent Axel is so cute right now.

Theodore shook his head fondly "Alright son. I'd love to stay and chat longer with you two boys but the CEO of Carter Spink owes me a rather large cheque for Warm Hands. Now you better visit me and bring Kendall along or I will be very unhappy with you for real this time."

"Alright dad." Axel promised.

"It was lovely meeting you Theodore." I said.

"The pleasure is all mine. I'm just glad my son is finally surrounding himself with good people." He stated before moving along.

I let out a big sigh "Your dad is really nice."

"There's nothing else he really can be." Axel said looking distracted for a second.

"So, you cried at the sight of cabbages as a kid?" I teased making my boyfriend groan out. "You can't really blame me. All vegetables are evil when you're a child."

"Aww now I know what to make for dinner tomorrow." I winked.

"My loved ones are turning against me. Please tell me you're joking." He frowned looking so cute that I couldn't help but peck his cheek quickly. It made me happy that he thought of me as a loved one, meaning I was dear to him. He was already one of the most important things in my life right now.

"Nope." I said popping the p.

"Hmm then I'll probably skip to desert then." He said in that voice he knew melted me like ice instantly. I wanted to smack him because we were in the midst of several people and it would not go great on my conscience desecrating his dad's house.

"You two better not orgasm here." A familiar voice brought my out of my daze.

It was Shorty looking like a goddess in a strapless white gown with tiny little diamonds sewed around it. Her hair was long and smooth running almost down her waist making me think of extensions because I knew for sure that it was shoulder-length. Though I preferred it that way.

"We're saving that for the car." Axel said rather boldly.

She rolled her eyes "Men."

"You look beautiful." I complimented her.

"Thanks Kendall. At least someone noticed." She glared at Axel. He gave her a bored look "Darling no one needs to tell you that. You've been breaking hearts since foetus."

"Thank you." Shorty gasped as if it were truly a compliment. "I've been running from an irritating marquee who seems to think I'm destined to bear his children all night." We all seemed to shudder at the thought for some reason.

"Wonder how poor Martin's doing." I remarked remembering the baroness who bought him.

Shorty scoffed "She's probably trying to hook him up with her grandson who's probably been single so long everyone assumes he likes cock. Won't be the first time though, blue bloods are really touchy when it comes to relationships."

"That's just tragic." I stated feeling bad for him.

Axel chuckled "She's going to be disappointed. Martin is an asshole to any other male who isn't Spencer and tried to hit on him."

"Um where's the bathroom?" I asked suddenly feeling pressed.

"Just by down the hall by your left love." He directed.

I followed his directions and found a wooden door which I assumed was the bathroom. Luckily it was vacant so no awkward encounters were in check. While I whistled the door opened startling me.

"It's occupied." I said over my shoulder hoping that the person heard me.

It closed and a sighed in relief that the person heard me even though I should have locked the door in the first place while I did my business.

But I turned, almost screaming to see Lauren staring intently at me.

"What are you doing here?" there was no hiding my surprise.

"Just wondering something." She said eyeing me a lot more now. I felt uncomfortable being alone with her since the space wasn't so big. Plus it's never really fun being alone with your boyfriend's ex. I wondered if Axel knew she was here even though I wouldn't be surprised if he didn't. He had said before that her parents knew his father before so it was expected for her to grace the occasion.

"You know I never really talk much." Lauren said as if this was the most normal situation in the world. "But now I just really want to know what's so special about you that Axel seems to like you so much."

"Look I don't think you want to start this." I stated nervously as she moved closer. Her tight red dress had a deep V cut which exposed her rather large bosom. Her perfume made my head spin simply because she was too close for my liking

"It's probably because you're younger." She said thoughtfully. "He never really had a thing for Americans though."

By now my back was pressed to the sink.

"I graduated with honours from Oxford University. I'm worth more in millions than you'll ever be in your life, so maybe it's a phase." She concluded. "He doesn't really mind as long as you've got a hole he put his penis in. But I'd like to warn you that in a matter of time Axel's going to come to his senses and get bored of. Just don't feel too disappointed when that happens."

Her words made me absolutely aggravated. How dare this bitch?!

I shoved her a little "Look lady, before you go into the whole cliché psychotic ex thing please understand that I genuinely like Axel and nothing will change that so if you're going to give the you'll ruin my life speech to scare me off, think again."

"I'm giving you an easy route out. You leave him then I'll settle you with whatever amount you want when we're married." She said as if a relationship was an item to be bought.

"Listen little boy." Lauren spat. "I may not have been with Axel recently but there is no way he'll ever replace me with someone as worthless as you."

"Then why are you worried?" I taunted. "If I'm worthless then why do you have to try so hard to intimidate me? I don't know exactly what went down with the two of you but he broke it off for a reason. Now I'd advise you to get over it and stay the fuck away from me because you don't scare me one itty bit."

She cocked her head to the side "You need proof? I'll give you proof."

Lauren shuffled in the small clutch and brought out a small brown envelope. "Here."

I snatched it eyeing her warily before seeing those words that shattered my world completely.

Miss. Lauren Calder has been tested and proven to be five months pregnant.

Happy belated New Year!

A lot of you thought that Axel getting auctioned would make Kendall mad. Why? I'm not sure.

Do you guys think Lauren is lying or not?

Chapter 19 - Knock You Down

For the next few days I slept in my apartment. My excuse to Axel was that I needed to study and didn't want to be in his space all the time. When I mentioned that it had to do with my academics he completely understood which made me feel even worse already.

After that night in the bathroom with Lauren I shut down completely. Axel tried asking me what the matter was but I didn't tell him and just allowed him assume that it was exam jitters. There was no way I could tell him. Every time I tried to open my mouth to say something I felt bile raise up my throat and felt the urge to puke my brains out.

I had no idea if he knew or not. If he did, why didn't he tell me? I never made him think that it was compulsory for him to tell me everything but this was important. Something within me questioned whether it was his child or not.

I remembered shouting at Lauren and asking her if the child was his. All she did was smile and told me to ask Axel.

Maybe that was why I didn't ask him yet.

I was afraid that she might be right. The somewhat sensible part of me knew Lauren was the ruthless type and would say anything to get what she wanted. But why was there this thing in me that wondered whether she was lying. Axel had refused to tell me details of their relationship. While I knew that he would never cheat on me, it was a possibility that something could have happened long before I came into the picture.

"Mate are you gonna murder the poor fork?" Pierce's concerned voice drew me out of my thoughts. Instead of eating I was fisting my plastic fork so hard it was already breaking a little. The seafood chow mien in front of me was untouched apart from a few nudges when I pushed it around before.

"Not really hungry." I stated dropping the fork and running my hands over my face.

"Normally you'd be trying to wrestle the egg rolls with me but you haven't even touched one. What's wrong Kenny?" He asked also dropping his own fork.

I shrugged "Studying's just taken a chunk out of my appetite I guess."

"Are you sure?" Pierce questioned further.

I sighed "Yes I am. I'm really not in the mood for an interrogation tonight."

"Ok." He mumbled even though he wasn't satisfied with my reply. Even Pierce seemed to be seeing someone judging by the late calls he received and unconscious grins while reading his texts nowadays.

I pushed my plate away and went to my room to see if I could get some more studying done. Luckily despite this issue I'd been able to study and write my exams without any difficulties. Whenever I study I'm able to shut out the world around me and do so. It only makes me a lot reluctant to close my textbooks and face the world around me.

The doorbell rang.

I waited for a little while but Pierce didn't go to check who it was. He was probably showering or in bed already.

I reluctantly dragged my ass from the desk in my room to check who it was. I opened to door to see Axel dressed in his suit and I knew that he'd come here straight from work.

"What are you doing here?" I tensed.

His gaze made me shudder "I'm sorry if it's turned to a crime to want to visit my own boyfriend. But I'll break the law anyway."

He walked inside and I didn't even have the strength to tell him not to.

"Now talk." He commanded.

I folded my arms "About what?"

"You know I hate it when you do this." Axel stated shoving his hands inside his pocket. "Act like there's something taunting you but deny any chance of help from me."

"There's nothing wrong with me I've told you."

"Then why have you been avoiding me?! And don't you dare say it's your exams because even when I offer to keep you company while you study you refuse. I've called you seven times this evening and you haven't even picked once. I was so worried that I didn't even go home to change like Timothy suggested instead I came over to see you and make sure that you haven't been hurt again. I drove here myself because I didn't want to keep him past his hours."

I sighed closing my eyes. He had no idea how guilty his actions made me feel. I refused to say anything but my uneasiness didn't go past him.

It made me torn between wanting to tell him and keeping it to myself because the fear in me was too great. Telling him felt like I would somehow acknowledge that deep down within me, Lauren's words hit home because I did feel like I wasn't good enough for him.

"Axel I-"

"Last time you refused to tell me what was happening to you. This time I'm not going to let it go." Axel said coming closer to me.

I bit my lip and placed my arm around his shoulder "I know." I leaned in until I was kissing him softly. He seemed surprised and maybe hesitant but reciprocated after a little while. For almost a week now I'd almost forgotten how it felt to have his lips on mine. He was heavily possessive and thrust his tongue into my mouth making me forget what my original dilemma was. I moaned as he held my waist and pressed my body on his without any intent to let go.

"Are you trying to distract me?" Axel pulled away breathing hard much to my displeasure.

"No." I replied.

"Kendall."

"I need you please." I begged wanting to forget everything else for a moment and lose myself with him. He kissed me tentatively before I jumped and wrapped my legs around his waist.

"My bedroom's to the right." I whispered sensually.

He moved us both blindly to my room before setting me down on the bed and letting lust over take over both of our senses completely.

******

Axel stroked my hair while spooning me from behind. Our sweaty and heavily sated bodies were intertwined together under the sheets as I basked in the hazy glow of post-sex. I enjoyed the feeling hoping that I would be able to push off the subject long enough. He pecked my shoulder trailing his lips down my spine and I bit down a moan.

"Don't think that I've forgotten what I was asking you."

I tried not to let out a disappointed gust of air through my lips. It seemed that there was no keeping this now.

"I'm serious Kendall. Tell me what it is." His tone was starting to sound demanding.

I curled my lip "When was the last time you met with Lauren alone?"

He shifted behind me "What?"

"You heard me."

"I can't exactly remember since I haven't had a reason to be alone with her all this while." Axel mused. "What does that have to do with anything?"

Carefully I turned to face him so that I could properly look him in the eye "When last did you sleep with her?"

He looked shocked "What-"

"Please answer the question Axel." I said as stoically as I could.

He was silent "A few months ago."

It felt like my heart was ripped out of my chest and tossed to a herd of animals. I couldn't move or react; my entire body went numb.

"You said you were broken up for a year." My voice was so undeniably shaky. Axel sighed "I was at a party she attended. I got drunk and I don't remember the details but the next morning I woke up to her in my bed. I was angry at her for moving on me since she knew that I was drunk. She apologized and said that she missed me but I shut her down. That was when I got her name removed from my private visitors list."

I played with my duvet "When exactly?"

He pursed his lips "Five months ago."

That was is. I couldn't keep the tears from falling down any longer. These past few days I'd been holding it all in. Now I couldn't anymore.

I cried holding the sheets to my face "She wasn't lying."

"Babe, what's wrong?" Axel asked heavily concerned. I shut my eyes "At the charity ball Lauren stalked me to the bathroom. That was when she told me that she was pregnant with your child. When I told her that she was lying she just told me to ask you."

I felt his body tense "W-What?"

"Lauren is pregnant with your child!" I finally shouted it out.

He looked taken aback "That's not possible."

"Well it is!" I sobbed "You fucked her and now she's pregnant with your kid. That's what's been troubling me all this time. Happy now?!"

"Shit." He sudden looked confused and overwhelmed at the same time running his hands through his hair "This is fucked up. I was drunk but I didn't think anything like this would happen."

"Well it did." I announced bitterly.

Axel looked at me with fear in his eyes "Kendall please, this shouldn't change anything between us."

I stared hard at him "You know that's not true. That woman might be carrying your child and you'll have no choice but to associate with her for that reason."

"But that doesn't mean that I don't want to be with you." He pleaded.

The already damp sheets were pressed on my chest. I hated her. I hated that woman so much for doing this to me. I was already deeply insecure without this happening to me. It seemed as though nothing good in my life was ever permanent.

Maybe Mara was right. Maybe I really don't deserve good.

After all it was my fault and my father's that our family was torn apart today.

"She's lying." Axel whispered sounding broken "Lauren has to be lying."

I sniffed refusing to look at him "I think you should go now."

"Kendall-"

"Just until after I'm done with my exams ok? I just need to focus on them for now." I assured him. His face dropped and it just broke my heart into two seeing him like this. But I had to do this for both of us.

I kissed his lips softly "I just want to be alone for now."

"Ok." His voice was so hoarse it was a miracle I heard him. It was hurting me too, it was hurting me so badly but there was no other option for now.

Because I had gone and stupidly fallen in love with Axel Gold.

I'm pretty sure 80% of you hate me now. But I want to bring to light that it's not always rainbows and butterflies in a relationship. My characters are human and react to situations the best way that they can. Kendall has always been super insecure even if he's never shown it so his reaction is streamlined with this.

Just keep that in mind yeah? I honestly appreciate you all and will try to update soon when I'm done feeling sad over my new school policy I just read online.

xx

Dreaded Authors Note

I'm so sorry guys, I personally hate doing this and I'm sorry if your heart jumped a little thinking this was an update but it's note. The truth is that my laptop got a little roughed up at the airport and now I need a new one.

My parents offered to send me money but like the stubborn airhead I am I said I'll do it myself but it's taking so long seeing as international student accounts do that (I school in Cape Town)

My boyfriend offered me his laptop but I really don't want to scar him with gay smut (he is too innocent with that cute blonde hair and those glasses to know what I write lol)

Anyways I'll try and update as soon as I can which might be a little late. But thank you guys for understanding my dilemma. Worst case I'll do two updates

xx

Chapter 20 - Wet Realities

Because I love you all so much I decided to update on my phone. My laptop is arriving by Monday or Tuesday hopefully (I paid so much for early shipping so it better) and my updates will be much faster then. This is probably short and I'm sorry for that. Hope you enjoy this chapter 'cause my thumbs hurt. P.S if it sucks my head is all over the place.xx

"You like that?" He whispered in the shell of my ear.

"Yes." I stated breathless much to his delight. Axel leaned away from me straddling my thighs "Hmmm, I wonder if I should just let you come now or wait a little longer."

"Please now." I begged knowing that it was more of a promise.

A wicked grin clouded his handsome features immediately.

"Fine."

The relief was evident.

He was a master at this game. Right now I didn't mind breaking a few rules as long as he ended up pleasuring me. Don't blame me; sex with Axel was worth jumping continents for.

Axel leaned down tantalizingly pressing his lips on my belly button. I shivered opening my mouth slowly as he trailed down slowly to the waistband of my boxers. He sucked indulgently on the skin there before staring at me with lust filled eyes.

"Will you do something for me babe?"

"Anything." I pleaded wanting him to take his lips down further.

"Wake up Kendall."

"What?" My face was scrunched up in confusion.

Suddenly I felt a pillow make contact with my face.

"Wake up Kendall!" I was assaulted again with the pillow.

I groaned both relived and annoyed that Pierce interrupted my dream once again. I knew people went through all manner of issues after a break-up or seperation but the one symptom no one told me about were the dreams.

Notice the plural because I'm pretty sure dreaming of Axel blowing me had been a regular occurence for close to two weeks now.

I know it seemed pathetic but it was only much needed proof how even my body craved so much for him.

"When I said you could sleep in my room I didn't sign up for this much moaning." Pierce complained as I threw the pillow down.

"Sorry man." I apologized rubbing my temple.

He sat on the edge of the bed "Honestly I get that you miss him."

I groaned not in the mood "Please don't start."

Pierce raised his hands in surrender "I only speak the truth. I would have been silent about if I didn't have to endure you revealing your deepest desires right beside me. Really, FOUR fingers?!"

I swore remembering that part quite well.

He sighed "Exams ended yesterday. Maybe you should call him now."

"And say what?" I growled annoyed.

"Sort out this while thing between yourselves. Make the bloody witch go for a paternity test." He suggested.

I sighed "M'not sure. She planned it so carefully so that she would get pregnant. And Axel is the kind of guy who would never abandon his own."

As much as the whole situation hurt, I couldn't help but admire that certain quality in him.

"Exactly, which means he isn't going to abandon you either." Pierce reasoned.

"But once the baby comes half of his attention's going to be divided. And Lauren is the mother so there is no way to ignore her at all." I finally voice one of my true concerns.

"But is Axel worth it?" Pierce asked surprising me. "Just ask yourself if with everything going on being with Axel is worth it in the end."

He stood up from the bed "I can't really do the whole therapist thing but I do know that once you answer that question you'll know what to do."

Pierce exited but not before adding "Who needs cable porn with you around?"

I managed to thrust a pillow at him despite my pity party.

******I couldn't help but maul over what Pierce said. Mostly because it was pretty true and I was not used to zen Pierce. My exams had finished so I was free mentally. Failure wasn't what scared me because I'd gotten a fair share of distinctions in the past.

I didn't have much to do really since unlike everyone else I didn't have a job keeping me occupied. I had a work-study program but the hours were rubbish so I depended on my scholarship and the transfers my mom sent each month. She was pretty generous since her job as vice president of a catering company had a pretty good salary. Mara worked at some fancy New York job while her fiance' was also a trustfund brat.

I never really had fancy stuff but my mom always made sure that I was comfortable.

My finger hovered over Axel's contact number on my phone. I didn't know whether to call him or not. I had no ideq if he would even want to listen to me at all. But one thing I failed to let my beloved roomate know was that I was in love with him. My dilemma wasn't that I thought he wasn't worth it.

It was that he would feel content with his new life and decide that I wasn't worth it anymore.

Against my better judgement I dialled his number. It rang for about two seconds before he picked up "Hello?"

Fuck he was voice was so raspy and raw and I had to hold myself not to burst into tears.

"Um it's me."

There was silence. "You've finally called me."

"I'm so sorry." My voice was so low even I couldn't believe it.

"I wanted to say that you're worth it." I bit my lip "Even with this you're still worth it."

"Do you mean that?" Anyone would be fooled with how cool his voice was. I could still sense the emotion in those words.

"Yes." I swallowed. I wanted to tell him thqt I loved him.

"Not seeing you for so long dampened me you know." Axel said and I rememberd how much I loved his voice. It wasn't even about his accent. The ability to deeply draw words only how he could.

"Me too." I said shyly not wanting to fixate on any of those dreams I'd been shamelessly having for a while.

"You're also worth it Kendall." He stated making my heart clench "I know that you doubt it but you truly are worth everything to me."

The tears that released themselves were too much to hold. This man, how had I lived before him? People always say that love at first sight doesn't exist. It may not be visible but that does not mean it isn't there. I've seen it already on my side and somehow on Axel's even if we'd only known each other a short time.

"There's something I have to tell you." He said.

I sniffed "What?"

There was a knock on my door interrupting us. Pierce was out with his new hidden "interest" since I managed to pry it out of him after a while since they seemed pretty serious about each other. But they were out so I had to open the door.

"I"ll call you back. Someone's at the door." I said reluctantly getting off the kitchen counter.

"Alright babe." Axel didn't sound happy making me suspect that what he wanted to say was important. But on the other hand I smiled inwardly that he called me by my usual pet name.

It made me even more irritated with whoever was distubing our moment.

I opened the door to reveal Lauren standing there.

"I know you might not want to see me but I think it's better if you do." She said clutching to her large white bag.

I wanted to slam the door on her face but decided to just listen to her out of sheer curiosity. "Five minutes."

Part of me wanted to call Axel and tell him that his baby mama was here. But our previous conversation was good and I didn't want to ruin the positive air around us. I would listen to whatever she had to based solely on the fact that she was the mother is his child. I respected him that much.

She walked into my apartment, her expensive wedges making noise on the hardwood floors.

"I wasn't sure where to park my car but I hope that it's safe." Lauren said sitting on the couch without invite.

I pursed my lips "Probably not." That was to irk her. "Now them me what you want. I'm not even going to ask how you found my apartment because the next time I see you the police will be contacted I promise. Now talk."

Her expression showed surprise but it was quickly concealed "Axel and I have talked and come to an agreement. I would also like the two if us to come to an agreement."

I remained quiet.

She brought out a piece of paper from her bag and placed it on the coffee table.

It was a cheque for £2000.

I stared hard at her "What is this for?"

"To compensate for any feelings you still have for him. Once the baby is born I can compensate you with more if it means you'll stay away from Axel." Lauren said briskly as if she didn't think I could say otherwise.

I pursed my lips "Isn't it pathetic that you have to wave money every time? Axel doesn't have to be with you to take proper care of his child. It's bad enough that you manipulated this whole situation to your benefit."

"It didn't-" She started but I cut her off.

"I know what happened. I know that you got into bed with him when he was drunk. You did this on purpose." I said calmly even though my emotions were anything but.

Lauren looked agitated "Don't talk to me that way."

"You can't really tell me what to do now Lauren. You're going to be in my boyfriend's life permanently now so. I'm willing to tolerate you but if you do what you just did again I'll I won't hesitate to make all your effort of staying close to my boyfriend worthless."

It wasn't my nature to threaten but Lauren probably brought out the worst in me.

"Your time is up." I announced "Get out."

Lauren took her sweet time getting up "You'll regret this. Not taking this deal now."

"I've got a sister who's ten times than you. You don't scare me at all."

And with that she left. I fished out my phone from my pocket wanting to get the details of this conversation from my head dialling Axel.

"Um Axel-"

"I was trying to tell you Lauren isn't pregnant. She lied."

Meh, probably short but don't blame me. Can't write on my phone for so long so consider this a record for me. I'm writing a new story called Check Mate which is also boyxboy and I already had the first chapter saved before my laptop git broken so all I need is a cover. If you guys can make one please don't be afriad to contact me or recommend anyone who you feel can.

Ciao!

Chapter 21 - Ad Infinitum

I'd like to believe that all my life I've made a string of well informed choices. From childhood I can proudly say that I've never been one to make a spur of the moment decision or do something utterly rash. If I was ever hungry as a baby I would wait until morning when my mother would come with my formula. Granted everyone was worried about me since I didn't cry too much like all normal kids did but my dad decided that it was my severely careful and patient nature.

But about two months ago when I decided toss caution to the wind by getting into a relationship with a man whose boat I trashed, I can confidently say that reckless is my middle name.

It sounded much better than Kendall Peter Ross anyway.

So that's why it wasn't too fazed with myself appearing in Axel's office only twenty minutes later after my phone call, barely out of breath after hearing the news that Lauren was indeed not knocked up.

"Um hi?" The red haired receptionist I'd known as Tricia gave me a confused look as I strutted past confidently in my grey sweats and matching tee shirt. I'm pretty sure it wasn't the fact that I looked like I just ran out of bed (which I did) but that I really didn't care.

It had only taken me two seconds to process the information before blinding grabbing my wallet and storming out of the flat without warning.

"Hi Tricia." I greeted her happily hopping into the elevator without giving any room for a reply. There was a woman in a white suit would looked like she would have cared less if I was a terrorist in a monkey suit. In all honestly I was flustered with too many emotions to really care. My main thoughts were revolving around the conversations which had taken place within the last 24 hours and what was going to happen right after now.

After the ping sound the elevator made indicating that I was on my desired floor, I stepped out nervously because even after my determined haste I really didn't know what to expect.

I walked right into Axel's office ignoring his secretary Stella who was protesting at her desk. I simply opened the door and shut it with a single glance at anyone else.

My eyes were fixed only on the dark haired Adonis who was in front of me with a look of slight confusion also clouding his features.

"Hi." I said looking down at the floor. Because two of not seeing Axel made me forgot how else to react.

"You're here." He said clearly enough for me to hear. I nodded "I am."

Stella burst into the room "I tried to stop him sir-"

"Leave Stella." Axel said lowly without taking his eyes off me.

She glanced at the both of us in confusion "But-"

"Remember that I pay you to listen to me. If you can't do that then I have no further need for you." He said calmly still burning holes in my skull. She nodded leaving the room without single word. My chest was pumping with too much anticipation to realize that I had just gotten someone threatened.

Axel walked towards me, making my heart tremble with every stride that he took. His hand pushed my chin up forcing me to look at him "Why did you come?"

"I missed you." I replied weakly feeling so desperate for his touch and not understanding his cool demeanour towards me.

The hand on my chin carefully moved to the nape of my neck caressing it gently. But he still didn't say anything.

"Lauren came to my apartment." I stated. "Just right before I came here. She tried to buy me off on the condition that I would leave you two alone."

Still no reply.

"I told her to go to hell." I whispered for some reason. "Because I can't stay away from you." At the moment I felt completely naked. Vulnerable was the right word. Like my soul had been ripped from my body and laid bare in front of his very eyes. It was a feeling I both loved and hated at the same time.

"You." Axel said while leaning down to my neck "Are mine Kendall. Every single bit of you belongs to me." I'll be the gum on your shoes if it means I'll be a part of you.

"You and I. We burn ad infinitum."

There it was.

I burned. Fuck being like this in his arms made burn. He was the gasoline to my flame. I whimpered when he pushed me to the wall roughly bruising my neck with hard kisses which was fine. It's not like I wanted him to go slow anyway.

"Shit, you have no idea how much I fucking missed you." Axel growled into my neck making me whimper out at the vibration. My legs were forced around his waist as he carried me to his large smooth mahogany desk and plopped me there without warning. Before I could recover my breath his mouth enveloped mine in a searing kiss.

The kiss reminded me of every emotion I had felt in the two weeks away from him. Fear, sadness, lust and wanting. But most importantly it reminded me exactly what he made me feel whenever he was around me. Care, happiness, security and completely real love.

That alone caused the first tear drops to fall from my eyes.

He pulled away stroking my cheeks with his thumb "Hey, what's wrong?"

I shook my head "I was stupid. I always run away at the first sign of any trouble because I'm scared. That's the only way I cope, by running. But I've realized now that even if I'm the world's biggest coward and you deserve to hate me for it; I'll never run away whenever it comes to you because you're worth it. Even if I have to fight or get hurt in the process I will because I can't stay away from you Axel. What we have makes me feel alive."

He kissed away my tears "You aren't a coward and I could never hate you. You came Kendall. Just promise me that no matter what happens we'll never be separated again. Lauren's test was forged by the way."

Even with my tears I couldn't help but snort at that.

"I'm going to ask about that in more detail but later." At the moment I just wanted to remain in his arms for as long as I could.

"We belong together Kendall."

I just nodded stayed buried in his chest for as long as I could enjoying the comfort he provided.

"I'm sorry I killed your boner." I said quietly making him rumble in laughter.

Axel kissed my forehead "Don't worry. I wasn't going to fuck you here love. We've been apart from far too long; I'll save it for when you're lying comfortably on my bed and you can scream as loud without worrying about being heard."

Is it bad that I missed his dirty mouth too?

"But I want to try kinky office sex too." I whined. He kissed my mouth once again "Probably when I fire Stella."

"Ad infinitum huh?" I mused running my fingers on his chest.

Axel pressed his hand on mine "To infinity. It's Latin."

I nodded seriously "Sounds sexy coming from you." He kissed me one more time pushing his all making it as passionate as ever. I wrapped my arms around his neck pushing him closer to me. I pulled away breathing hard before latching my lips on his neck "I've been going crazy without you."

He groaned as I tried to work up a mark. "Sorry babe still got meetings today and I don't want the upper heads to get suspect I've been playing hooky with you."

I giggled at the word hooky because really?

He rubbed the purplish mark on his neck "I've created a sex crazed incubi haven't I?"

I snorted "Like anyone would resist banging that hot body of yours stud."

"Hmm, way to make me feel less like hooker." He rolled his eyes but anyone could see the arrogance rolling off his shoulders.

This man. Everything he did only reminded me how much I loved him.

And fuck I loved him.

"I love you so much." I blurted out. There was no embarassment or fear in my words. Just truth.

Axel kissed my lips one more time "No you can't."

That was a stab to my gut.

He caressed my cheek "Because I love you more Kendall Ross."

Thanks for being super patient with me guys. Check out my other story Check Mate because the synopsis is up and I'll start posting chapters soon enough. I'm so sleepy so enjoy your update

xxx

Chapter 22 - Real And True

This is a sex heavy chapter and I am totally not ashamed. Thanks to those who checked out my new story Check Mate and to all of you still reading this story even when I feel like my writing isn't as good as most writers on this site. I'm really grateful to everyone.

Now I'll shut up and let you read ;)

"Do you have anywhere to be?" Axel asked pressing soft kiss to the column of my neck. I bit my lips forgetting what I was supposed to say for a while.

"No, and even if I do fuck it."

We had moved to his apartment after I had waited in his office so he could attend his board meeting. Stella seemed to give me the stink eye when we were leaving but I was too happy to pay any attention to her anymore.

I lay contently on the couch with Axel spooning me from behind. He had changed into a navy blue t shirt and gym shorts. His lips made constant contact with the back of my neck causing me to let out little noises of approval. We were tangled into each other just lying there for hours without any disturbance. Our intimacy was completely platonic but I didn't care. Just being in his arms was enough for me.

Bliss was the only way that I could describe the moment.

"Can I say something?" I asked biting my lip.

"Of course." He replied.

"I love you." I said truthfully. Now that it had been gone over with I could stop saying it every chance I got. I didn't want Axel to end up ripped away from me once again without knowing how much I loved him.

"I love you much more." He kissed our intertwined fingers. "And nothing will change that."

"How did you know Lauren lied?" I asked placing my head on his bicep. I had wanted to avoid the subject much longer and just enjoy being back with Axel for the moment but my curious nature was getting restless with each second.

He sighed, allowing me to realize that he also wanted to out this off much further also "I asked her to verify with a doctor but she refused to. She showed me the test and wanted me to rely on just that but I insisted and so she went."

"But she wasn't pregnant?" I finished for him.

He shook his head "The doctor explained that she had pseudocyesis - a false pregnancy. He explained that because she wanted a baby so badly her body had created the illusion that it was carrying a child but it wasn't."

Wow, that was unexpected.

"So she wanted a baby all this time?" I questioned.

He pursed his lips "Lauren wanted to have my baby for the sole purpose of getting me back. She got into my apartment that night for that alone."

At this point my disgust had morphed into pity. Pity for a woman who went through such extremes, just to keep a man who had no feelings for her. It was pity-worthy from my point of view.

"I'm thinking of getting a restraining order against her." He mused running his fingers through my back.

"She came to my apartment this afternoon." I remembered "I still don't know how she found out my address." It worried me slightly knowing that she could easily find my location. Lauren's actions had proved that she was somewhat ruthless and I wouldn't put anything above her though.

"She'll never hurt you I promise." Axel assured rubbing my shoulder.

"I'm mad, but at the same time I feel bad for her." I whispered to him. Maybe her reasons for wanting Axel were genuine. Maybe somehow she really did love him in her own way at the end of the day. But she went about it the wrong way hurting people to get that. Yes I may sound like a hypocrite for believing that if you love something let it go because there was no way I was letting Axel go. But just a few weeks ago I thought it would be the right thing for both of us.

He sighed once again "I don't want to talk about her right now." I nodded understanding his plight completely.

"Well the only way you're having kids is through me." I said suggestively.

Axel looked utterly amused "Really? How do you plan on doing that?"

I shrugged "We'll find a way."

He pushed me so I was lying on my back with a predatory smile on his face. My eyes widened as he placed soft kisses on my stomach "Why don't we start now?"

"Hmm." I agreed kissing him back hotly on the mouth. We kissed slow and dirty for a few minutes before Axel pulled away without warning.

I whined at the loss of contact but he held me down "There's something I want to show you."

I quirked an eyebrow "What is it?"

He stretched his hand "Come with me."

He led me through his obscenely large penthouse. I once had the privilege of taking a tour around and was impressed by the amount of space he had. Axel led me through to one of the two guest rooms and opened the door for me. I was confused seeing as this room was completely bare apart from some essential furniture. It made me wonder what was so special that he wanted to show me.

"What did-"

I stopped abruptly fully taking in the image before me. It was Martin's painting from the exhibit, the very same one I fell in love with from first sight and felt broken after learning that it was bought already.

"How? But it was sold and the first to get sold in fact and, and-" I rambled off as Axel wrapped his arms around my waist. Something silenced me.

"That was you. You bought it didn't you?"

He quietly kissed my forehead "Yes I did." I could feel my throat tighten and the overwhelming sense of love running through my veins. Just when I thought I couldn't love him anymore, he proves me wrong.

"I saw how you looked at it that night. The way your eyes shone captivated me instantly." He confessed, whispering the words to my ears. I swallowed fighting the huge lump in my throat.

"That was the first time I knew I loved you, even if I didn't say it." IlovedyouIlovedyouIlovedyou-

He held me closer "You're one of a kind Kendall. When I see you I don't see male or female, all I see is you."

A warm kiss was pressed behind my ear. I sobbed "It's scary. It's scary how hard I've fallen for you because I love you and it hurts my heart so much. What scares me is that I'm going to wake up one day and realize that this is just a dream because this is just too perfect to be real. But I want this to be real because I don't ever want to lose you."

He held me to his chest "You won't lose me love. I'm here for you."

With Axel, I've learnt that loving someone doesn't take years to realize. When you're in love with someone it's there and it doesn't need to take a century to see. I had known Axel for a few months but everything within my being screamed love for this man. He consumed me from the inside out and taught me that maybe I was worth loving back.

My thoughts were interrupted when his lips met mine for an earth shattering kiss. I wrapped my arms around his neck pushing our bodies closer together desperate for contact. His hands roamed around me as though he was trying to memorize every single part of my body.

I moaned feeling his hardened member pressed against my thigh. Axel swore cupping my ass "I want you."

"Yes." I begged not wanting to waste any more time. He took his shirt off and chucked it somewhere in the room that none of us took any notice of. I ran my hand all over his strong heavily tatted chest just wanting to take in the unearthly feel of my man. And yes he was my man. My man, and no one else's.

Axel pushed me back on the wall helping me take off my pants. He tore off my grey shirt and bit my bottom lip in an aggressive kiss right before I could complain. I was now hard and dripping pre-cum on the hardwood floors. He kissed my neck all the way to my torso while I just let out little sounds of appreciation watching him go at it eagerly.

"Wait. Wanna suck you." I breathed out.

Axel pushed down his shorts with lightning speed. I had to stop myself from cumming right there after seeing him completely commando.

"Can you take all of me?" His voice was heavy with lust and emotion. I hummed getting on my knees and enjoying the fine specimen of the man before me. He leaned back on the wall and spread his legs to accommodate me.

I teased his tip with my tongue enjoying the way he hissed in pleasure. My body tingled watching the expressions on his face as I sucked eager taking all of him in my mouth.

"Fuck, oh my- just fuck." He swore hitting his head back on the wall as he held my hair and pushed himself even deeper into my mouth.

"So hot." he moaned bucking his hips deeper into my throat. Lord knows that I was gagging seriously but just seeing him vulnerable and open and true like this made it all worth it.

Saliva dribbled down my chin as he began to thrust in faster, utter a few inaudible words before shooting down his load into my throat. In my previous encounters that alone would have disgusted me but I swallowed every single thing happily just because it came from him.

Axel leaned down gently on the wall with his chest heaving. He looked exhausted and my chest swelled with pride at his wreckage.

"Come here." He said softly. I crawled to his side pressing my head on his neck and placing a soft kiss there.

"You undo me." he said still in daze. His hand ran down my back to the curve of my ass and I threw my head back when his middle finger found its way to my tight pink passage. It went in knuckles deep and teased around before he pulled out. I pushed my ass out to signal him that I wanted some part of him back in me now. But he deliberately didn't oblige.

Axel chuckled massaging my butt "I could build a shrine to your ass alone."

Well I was touchy because he wasn't doing much to worship it at the moment.

He knelt behind me pushing my ankles back over his shoulders. He pushed me down so that I was lying flat on my stomach. The floor was cold but my brain was too fried to really care anyway.

He kissed my spine down to the curve separating my cheeks slightly.

"So pretty." He muttered right before diving his tongue inside. I screamed.

I screamed so loud that for a moment I wondered whether all that sound really came from puny little me. His beard scratched the back of my thighs as his tongue did all kinds of things to me and I moaned shamelessly enjoying it all.

"AxelAxelAxelAxel-"

I babbled on and on as my brain seemed to remember nothing else. At that very moment all I knew and breathed and lived was Axel and him alone. Even till this day I maintain that only he could completely fuck the intelligence out of me.

"You're so hot. Oh fuck me please." I whined as he twirled his tongue over the sensitive part of my rim.

All he did was hum as though he was enjoying a particularly tasty treat and didn't want to let go of it any time soon.

"Cum for me." He said dangerously knowing that I was oh so close. I saw white as hot spurts of semen poured from me painting the floor completely. I took in a deep breath giving time for my body to come out of its sensitive orgasmic state.

But my eyes widened when I felt him press his hardened member on my thigh "Oh I'm not done with you yet."

Fuck.

My dick shot up faster than a NASA rocket and I had just come.

His tip was positioned in front of my hole "I'm losing my mind over you Kendall."

Then he began fucking himself fast and hard inside me. There were no condoms or lube; it was bare, raw and real. The final assurance of how much we trusted each other if we were both willing to open ourselves before each other.

Axel interlocked our hands together and kissed my neck while mutter words like "Mine" "Oh love" "So hot for me" and "I fucking love you".

I answered with "Yes" and "Please" and "Love you" every single time. The moon shone through the wall to ceiling windows and I couldn't help but glance at Axel and admire how beautiful he was to me. Not guarded or intimidating, just real.

With one final thrust we both came together. He howled (which was really sexy by the way) pouring every bit of his essence into me while my own cum pooled underneath me. He rolled off my back still dragging me to lay my head on his chest. I kissed his throat muttering words like "Sogood" "Iloveyou" "Bestsexever" in my hazy state.

His semen dripped from my asshole but I couldn't find it within myself to feel disgusted. I'd probably worship shit as long as it came from Axel.

He rubbed my back lovingly "No matter how many times I say it this, it won't ever feel enough. I love you."

"And I love you." I didn't add the too because it would only make me feel like I was repeating after him. I truly loved him whether he loved me back or not.

"Urgh I'm positive you've knocked me up." I complained shuffling my legs on the floor. His chest rumbled with laughter "I hope so. Wouldn't want anyone to doubt my virility."

I rolled my eyes but cuddled closer to him. We both gazed at the painting in the room.

"So do you want to take it back to your apartment?" He questioned running his fingers through my damp hair.

"No, you're part of me so I'm leaving it here. That way I can leave something of mine with you." I explained. He nodded slowly "I want you to move in with me."

That surprised me. "Really?"

Axel gazed at me "I want you to be around me every single time. I could pay off your lease so that Pierce wouldn't have to struggle with the rent. I'd even let you redecorate it any time you want."

I bit my lip.

"Hey." He said softly "You don't have to say yes now. I just wanted you to know."

I was glad. It wasn't that I wouldn't say yes, but I still needed time to properly process things over. I still pride myself in some of well laid out planning.

"I know you're gonna say I'm old, but we should probably get to the main bedroom before my back starts hurting." He suggested.

"Hmm, feeling lazy." I muttered latching onto him like a koala.

"That's why you have a hot strong boyfriend to carry you up." He said gathering me in his arms.

"Yay." I said tiredly. Axel carried me to the main bedroom still latched onto him. I felt relief once my back touched the soft bed and sighed when he spooned me from behind kissing his favourite place behind my ear. We were sweaty with dried cum all over our bodies but at this point my body was too worn out to care.

Axel's Blackberry rang annoying me immensely. I wanted to kick whoever was trying to disturb our lovely moment.

He sighed reluctantly untangling himself from me. "Don't go." I said selfishly wanting him to myself.

"Could be an emergency babe." He said already pushing away the sheets but I was persistent and held him down to the bed.

Axel let out a sigh "Do you really want a fire or something over your conscience because you didn't let me pick up the phone?"

He sounded both amused and annoyed.

I shrugged defiantly "I had mind blowing sex with you so the world could end for all I care."

He kissed the back of my neck chuckling lightly "Fine, just let me check the caller ID and be sure."

He did so dropping the phone right back on the bedside lamp "It's just Shorty. I'll listen to whatever she has to say tommorow."

I sighed contently when Axel wrapped his arms around and we both fell asleep with everything exactly the way it should be.

Are our lovebirds moving in together???????? Do you think it's the right choice or should Kendall wait a little more?

I value your comments so don't hesitate to paste them below

xxx

Not An Update But Important

H ey guys I know you must all be mad at me for the lack of updates but believe me it's not my fault. I'm trying to balance a new school, living in a different place, making time for meaningful relationships and I'm trying the best I can at life right now.

I love writing and all but lately I've been too choked up to even think of picking up my laptop to update. I'm trying to clear up my schedule but hopefully within the next 2-3 days I won't be as busy. Please if you have the time, see that I have altered the ending of chapter 22 a little to accomodate what I have in mimd for the next chapter.

Thank you guys for being so patient with me despite all.

Chapter 23 - Green Eyed Dilemma

Aghn! I managed another update in my super crazy schedule. Thanks for being super patient guys and I'm sorry this chapter isn't so long but I needed it that way to fit exactly with the plans I have for the next part. Enjoy and sorry for any mistakes (I wrote this under duress)!

"Remind me why what evil powers you used to lure me here again?" I asked Martin as we both sat down Buddha style in the middle of his and Spencer's huge room closet. Since my final exams were done and I had no classes, I had a lot more free time on my hands.

We had gone to watch a movie, had lunch and he gave me a tour of their impressive four bedroom townhouse. And somehow we ended up sorting clothes in his closet.

He rolled his eyes arranging a pair of shoes "Just shut up and pass me those hangers."

I groaned passing his the two hangers beside me. Honestly when he wasn't so focused on his art or gushing over anything related to Spencer, he was sort of a diva. But he was Martin so it was still cute on him.

"Why do you have such a huge ass closet anyway?" I asked sitting up straight. Martin looked focused on folding a multi-coloured scarf "Because Spencer has so many suits and he likes them spaced and organized."

"Really?"

He nodded "I could care about having so much space less really, but sometimes I wonder if he's got OCD. He's too coordinated and organized sometimes and it annoys the hell out of me. Can't deal with a single hair out of place." Despite his irritated tone you couldn't really miss the fondness in his voice.

I sighed "Well at least the only thing Axel bitches to me about is picking up my shoes."

Martin turned to look at me with a bright smile "I'm so happy for you guys. All loved up and ready to move in together." I told him all about our love confessions, even though I left out the part about Lauren and the fake pregnancy. It just didn't feel right to expose her like that even if she somehow seemed to deserve it.

"I'm not sure about the moving in part yet. Still thinking about it." I admitted.

He frowned a little "Oh, what's the wait?"

I sighed "Well I don't really know. I love Axel and I really do want to spend every single day with him but something within me is just holding me back."

"Sweetheart that's just your subconscious being pessimistic." Martin concluded now folding a bunch of ties into a drawer. "Moving in together is probably the biggest stage in a relationship and I understand how that might frighten you a bit."

I shook my head "It's just....I've never felt the way I feel for him for anyone else before. It just feels as though if I try to grasp it everything's going to evaporate so quickly. It's like once we move in together everything's been glued shut for good and that somehow scares me."

Martin gave me a sympathetic look "That's the thing about being in a serious relationship. I understand exactly how you feel." He dropped the last folded tie in the drawer.

"When Spencer and I got together, I moved in with him early on in our relationship. It was mostly because I wanted to get away from my parents but later I started feeling paranoid. For a moment I almost backed out because I thought we did everything too fast and we weren't going to last." He sighed running his hands through his hair with a small smile.

"But it turned out that I was scared for nothing. My advice would be for you to think about it properly, but at the same time don't back out of anything because you're afraid of jinxing it. Chances are that it will be the best decision you've ever made."

The honest truth was that I really did love Axel. Maybe Martin was right and my nerves were just getting the best of me. But it probably wouldn't hurt to still think over it a little bit more right?

"Thanks for the advice." I said with a half-smile. He shook his head "My pleasure. At least you came to me before Shorty. That girl thinks she'll steal my match-making crown."

"What a crown it is indeed." I commented while muffling a laugh which in turn caused him to flip me off.

Martin scoffed chucking a blue dress shirt on the floor "Really? He still kept this shirt after I told him it looked terrible? That man and his questionable fashion sense."

I rolled my eyes smiling. He was really one to talk.

******

"Hey love." Axel's voice always made me tingle in all the right places. That deep smooth tremor of his voice managed to make my heart skip no matter what I was doing. It never got old.

I pressed the phone closer to my ear shuffling down the cereal aisle at Asda "Hey babe. Aren't you supposed to be in a meeting or something now?"

"I just got out of one. Why, are you getting tired of me already? Got another man on the side?" He teased lightly.

"Wow you've discovered my secret. I'm fucking Martin on the side but don't tell Spencer please." I said dryly.

There was some shuffling at the background "I hope he bottoms. No one touches that butt of yours but me."

Typical.

I grabbed the box of Frosted Flakes and stuffed into my half full trolley. "You know it babe."

"But seriously where are you now? Are you still with Martin?" He asked.

"Just getting some groceries. Before I left this morning I looked into the pantry and the sight was not pretty." I explained pushing my trolley.

"Did Martin drive you there?" He asked.

"No Spencer came over and he got occupied." The thought gave me shivers and I definitely did not need the image of them going at it in that very same forsaken closet.

"You should have told me. I'd call Timothy to drive you." Axel now sounded slightly displeased. Oh my protective bear of a boyfriend.

"I'm fine. It's not so far away from the apartment anyway." I supressed the urge to roll my eyes. I understand his point of view but I was nineteen years old for goodness. It only seemed logical that I was more than capable of going grocery shopping without Timothy acting as my glorified babysitter.

"Still, I'm not comfortable with you out like that."

"Axel it's alright. I'm at the supermarket not Afghanistan." I argued.

He sighed "I honestly hate you being alone by yourself. Every time I can't help but remember when you got hurt-"

"Axel it's ok." I said firmly making sure he didn't finish that sentence. "Nothing major happened to me anyway. Just stop torturing yourself by thinking about that."

It annoyed my how much he let that loom over like a dark cloud over his conscience. I just needed him to understand that my getting hurt was not his fault in anyway and he didn't foresee it when I got out of the car that night.

"Right sorry. It's just a second nature of mine to always worry about you."

God, I loved him so much. My wonderful, handsome but sometimes annoyingly martyr of a boyfriend.

"And I want to kiss you so much for that." I said greeting an old lady with a smile on my way to the checkout counter. "But I swear that I'm fine."

"Ok. But the moment you aren't you'll let me know right?"

It's so funny how once upon a time this man scared that crap out of me. How he just seems like an eager little puppy most of the time. The transition is hilarious.

"Yes Axel I promise." I stretched out "Now I have to pay so I'll see you when I get home Batman."

"Batman?" I could hear the amusement in his voice "I might be Batman but you're the one I'd rather see in tights love."

The line went disconnected and my cheeks were blazing. Damn him.

"Cash or card?" The checkout girl asked me brightly. I quickly whipped out my Master card and handed over to her. After a while she gave me a small frown "I'm sorry sir but your card has been declined."

"What?" I asked confused.

She gave me an apologetic look "I'm sorry but that's what it says right here." There must have been some sort of mistake. My mom sent me some money only last month.

"Can I try it again?" I asked her and she nodded. However after two more tries the result was still the same.

"I'm sorry sir but I have other customers." She said sympathetically. I brought out my wallet "It's fine I'll just pay with cash."

"That'll be £90 please." She stated. That was a pretty chunky amount but it was a good thing that I went to the ATM earlier. I paid her and packed my stuff still flabbergasted about why my card wasn't working. I'll probably make a call to the bank and ask them what was going on. Maybe it was a network problem or something.

I got on the bus hauling my grocery bags inside. Suddenly it didn't seem like such a bad idea to get picked up, I thought as I squished myself between two girls. One of the girls was wearing heavy eyeliner and listening to music so loud that I could hear it right beside her even though she had her earphones on.

I wanted to tell her to tone it down but her blank stoic expression told me that she might not appreciate it at all. I sighed in relief when we reached the stop and I got off still clutching my grocery bags tightly. I walked a few blocks until I reached the front of the familiar apartment building.

"Evening Kendall." Hans the doorman greeted.

"Good evening Hans." I greeted back not looking at my front and bumping into someone as a result.

"Shit, I'm the so sorry." The person apologised as I bent over to pick up my stuff from the floor. Thankfully nothing spilled or broke. I smiled without looking up at who it was "It's fine really."

I looked up finally to get a complete shock "James?" I was not expecting to see my university friend here of all places.

"Kendall." He also sounded equally surprised. "Fancy bumping into you here."

"Yeah." I said looking around nervously. "What are you doing here? Or do you live here?"

"Gosh no. I came to see my uncle about some family stuff." He explained eyeing my curiously "What are you doing here?"

I shuffled my feet "Oh uh my boyfriend lives here. And I'm here for the time."

"Oh." I couldn't help but noticed how deeply disappointed he sounded with my answer. Strange.

"That's nice. I sort of got the impression that you were single again." He said slowly. I scrunched up my eyebrows in confusion "Where did you get that impression from?"

He scratched the back of his head "Uh Pierce told me last week that you guys were taking a break or something." Suddenly it seemed like a good idea to Taser Pierce in the butt until he promised to never spill out the details of my personal life to other people.

I let out an annoyed noise "We were but now we're back and I assure you very much together."

He mumbled something under his breath "I can see why."

"What's that supposed to mean?" I asked offended. What the hell was he implying?

James shook his head as if annoyed about something "It's just that a little while ago you acted like you couldn't stand him and suddenly you're dating and all over him. I mean that Pierce told me he's some hotshot millionaire or something-"

"Excuse me?" I screeched not sure whether I was more annoyed by what he said or the fact that Pierce really did seem to have no filter. "What are you trying to say? That I'm only with him for his money or what?"

James was normally a nice guy but right those were not the thoughts what passed through me at all. I knew that most people would think that but I never expected someone like him to throw in my face that I'm only with Axel for his money.

He was supposed to be my friend.

"No not like that Kendall." He stated quickly "I know that you aren't like that but somehow with the way you've gotten with him so quickly it just kinda…..looks that way."

"It just looks like I suck his dick for money." I said flatly not even believing the words coming out of his mouth.

James hesitated "That's not what I mean Kendall. I just don't get why you're with him."

If I was surprised before, I was completely and utterly flabbergasted now.

"I'm sorry I didn't get your holy seal of approval first James. Really I don't know why you even care, it's not like we were real friends. Half the time you don't acknowledge my presence unless Pierce forces me to hang out with you guys. It's not even worth it to try and justify my relationship with Axel to you because if you could say something like that, then you're not worth the time I'm using to talk."

Honestly it seemed like a one in a million chance for me to talk to James like this especially since I harboured a crush on him all that time, but anyone who dared question my love for Axel deserved to hear me lash out like a dragon.

I could tell that James was really surprised by my reaction.

"Hey that's not what I meant." He said a bit softer now grabbing my hand. "It's just long and complicated to begin with-"

"I thought you were home earlier." Axel's deep smooth voice made my heart do a double take in my chest.

I quickly pulled away from James' touch "Hey babe. I did but got held up after bumping into an old friend."

Axel slowly strode to my side eyeing James "Right. I think I've seen you before." His hands slithered around my waist in what I assumed were both want and possessiveness.

"Yeah I was just in the area but I'm on my way now anyway. I'll see you around Kendall." He said with a shaky smile before darting past us.

I brushed the feeling I got to the side "I should probably carry these up before the milk turns into cottage cheese."

"Do all your friends ogle you like that?"

One look from Axel and I knew that I had a lot to explain.

Fuck.

Who think's Axel is a cute little munchkin under that super hot, powerful aura of his? I know I do!

Vote and Comment my lovelies!

Chapter 24 - Falsetto

✱ Hides behind pillar* so sorry for the long update guys. School and life have had me too busy to even breath. But I do hope that you enjoy this super short update. So sorry and love you guys.

How come every time I leave you, you always end up having some wild crazy celebratory sex with the royal hottie over there?" Pierce chided over the phone.

It was just 7am in the morning and he already had me rolling my eyes. I pressed my thumb to turn off the coffee maker since it had been brewed to my satisfaction. Exactly how I knew Axel also liked it.

"I'm serious.

It's like every time you guys have an argument or you're sad, I turn my back for 2 seconds and wham - you're getting laid and I'm just hearing about it." I proceeded to

face the stove were I was frying some pancakes and turned on my speaker so that

I could focus on flipping my pancakes. "Last time I checked, I'm not a pornstar so my sex life isn't supposed to be public knowledge."

"Pfft don't ruin this for me." ever the dramatic one.

"By the way I bumped into James yesterday at Axel's building." I said grimacing when I

remembered our bittersweet encounter. It still made me skin prickle when I remembered how he had indirectly portrayed me as a gold digger. Those words still stung deeply.

"What exactly did you tell him about Axel and I?"

He cleared his throat "Oh I just told him that you were seeing someone when he asked. He

seemed pretty persistent on knowing who so I told him about Axel."

"Then what did you say about his profession?" I enquired further placing a perfect crisp

golden brown pancake on the plate beside me.

"Just that he was kind of rich but you guys were completely in love. Kind of weird the way he kept probing for questions if you ask me." He answered.

I sighed and turned off the stove "Look Pierce you're a great friend and all but could you

like refrain telling people about rich my boyfriend is? I love him and I'm not

sure Axel would be completely comfortable knowing that I spew out his status. I

know you mean well but just……stop it yeah?"

Pierce was silent for a while "It's cool mate. I'm sorry when I think about it it's pretty insensitive of me and I guess I should protect your privacy."

I let a breath "Thanks you're a great friend." Even though his mouth ran longer than the

English Channel, Pierce always stuck with me during everything. He really was a

great guy.

"Obviously." He sounded smug "Who else would apply balm on your butt after a one night stand gone wrong?" He promised that he would never bring it up again that stupid

idiot.

I groaned "I take it back. You're the worst. I hate you."

He cackled in delight "Sweetheart you love me. Stop lying to yourself you bloody American."

I rolled my eyes again "Why am I friends with you again?"

"Because I'm that one crazy perverted friend we are all supposed to have." he said creepily.

And that was surprisingly accurate. "Would love to chat but it would appear

that my beau is here right now."

"You know I'm yet to know who this mysterious guy is — hello? Pierce you there?" The fucker actually cut the line on me. Ha guess he wanted to keep his new guy a mystery for a little while longer.

But my thoughts were interrupted when I felt two strong arms wrapped around my waist.

I smiled involuntarily and covered his hands with mine "Look who's awake. Good

morning."

Axel buried his nose in my shoulder "Hmm, you smell so good love. And good morning to you too."

He kissed my neck before pulling away reluctantly to behold the feast I had set out. "Did a

fairy gift us with breakfast this morning?"

"Ha ha." I said sarcastically placing his plate of pancakes and bacon along with the fresh

coffee on the breakfast bar. "Just felt like making you breakfast for once."

He sat down on the breakfast bar "And I suppose all this wonderful food is in exchange for my silence about why that boy was eyeing you up again?" that wasn't my real reason for cooking breakfast but part of me did hope that he wouldn't bring it up. My encounter with James was both confusing and annoying and part of me really didn't want to remember it.

I bit my lip placing my own food on the bar and sitting "That wasn't my reason but I was

sort of hoping that you wouldn't bring it up."

Axel's jaw twitched. That wasn't a good a sign. "What was he doing here?"

I twisted my fork "He said he was visiting an uncle of his or something. I honestly don't

care. I just bumped into him a few minutes before you came."

I honestly hoped that he would believe me. Not that Axel had any issues trusting me or anything, but I knew that a situation like might annoy him. He was somehow entitled to be jealous after all. If I was honest, it made me squeal internally that he was jealous over me. The only funny thing was that James was utterly straight and had no interest in me.

"You're so clueless aren't you?" He sounded bemused.

"About what?" I asked.

Axel shook his head looking down at the bar before tilting his head sideways at me "That boy has it hard for you Kendall."

Wait, what?!

I blinked "That's not possible. James is straight."

He scoffed "I'm not saying that he isn't. I'm just saying that he obviously has a thing for you." did the lack of sex last night mess with him or something? Because there was no other theory other than that for Axel to come up with such crazy results.

"Think about it. His concern comes off exactly the way a jealous boyfriend would." He explained to me.

"But that's not how you act when youre jealous." I countered.

Axel sighed "Love you've never actually seen me jealous. Mostly because I know that you're mine alone and no one can change that. There are times when I do get a little anxious because I prefer not to see some certain people around you." His pointed look clearly meant that he was referring to James. "But no love I'm not jealous. Now your friend James, is steaming with jealously."

I chewed thoughtfully "I still have a hard time believing that. I mean before you came into the picture he never acted this way. Hell, it took us three encounters for him to remember my name really."

He sipped his orange juice "Maybe it took my coming into the picture to realize what a catch you are."

I rolled my eyes "Yeah right."

We ate in silence for a little longer since I really didn't feel like talking about James anymore.

"Have you thought about it?" Axel asked me quietly helping me pack up the plates.

"What?" I asked.

He dumped them into the sink before turning to me "I asked you to move in with me Kendall. And I'm waiting for you to reply me. I may not be a jealous man but I'm not very patient."

I curled my lip folding my hands across my chest "I sort of need more time to think over that. I know my answer already, but I need to fully justify it to myself."

He looked away "I'm trying my best not to force you into anything or pressure you. But you need to understand that I also have feelings and needs." He held my arms and pulled me towards him "Kendall.....I didn't ask you to move in because I want sex all the time."

My lips twitched slightly at that "That might be a bonus, but it's mainly because I don't want to be away from you. I love you and love waking up to you and I love seeing you wear my clothes when you cook and I love how you never seemed to keep your shoes properly even though I've told you a million times. I love all those things and maybe I'm selfish but I really don't want them to stop."

I was now smiling pretty brightly now.

"I also want that too. But I just need to get some things sorted first." I explained to him.

Axel nodded, then kissed my forehead "I love you so much." Then kissed my nose, and cheeks and jaw before finally moving to my lips. My back was pressed on the fridge as Axel feasted the hell out of my mouth. I could never get tired of kissing him. We pulled away slightly breathless, just staring hopelessly at each other.

I sighed melting into the wonderful feeling in his arms "And I love you. Now move so that I can do the dishes."

He patted my butt playfully "Get to work woman."

I scoffed "The whole point of this relationship is strictly no vagina."

He smirked "Especially not with an ass like that."

Walking in my apartment complex felt strange. Maybe because I had spent too much time in my boyfriends place. I'll admit that his expensive penthouse was pretty swanky, but for some reason I felt a lot more at home than at the place where I had been living for nearly a year.

The key thing was that Axel lived there. I'm sure that even if he resided in a cardboard box it would still feel like home to me. My boyfriend was currently at home after I convinced him to stay and catch up on some rest. The poor thing had been working non-stop this week and needed rest. I only came to get a few of my stuff before going back to the penthouse. Timothy was off to see his family so I took the bus instead, which was a relief. I'm pretty sure that Timothy and I had come a long way in our relationship, but it would be hard to work out our first meeting. The man nearly dumped me in the ocean for goodness sake.

I zipped up my jacket walking up the staircase, then freezing instantly when I saw how was sitting at my doorstep waiting.

James.

He spotted me immediately "Kendall I-"

"Save it." I cut him abruptly. "What are you doing here? Isn't it enough that you insulted me back at my boyfriend's place?"

He shook his head looking desperate "No it's not like that. I'm sorry for what I said back there."

"How did you know I was coming?" I questioned.

He shrugged "I didn't really. A lucky guess?" I moved past him into the apartment and shoved my keys into the keyhole. "We might as well have this talk inside. It's cold out here."

The apartment was warm and clean surprisingly. Looks like Pierce had been cleaning more than usual. Probably to impress his new boy toy. James sat on the couch opposite me.

I sighed "What is your deal anyway dude? Why are you so invested in my relationship?"

James looked down "I-I don't know. It doesn't feel right Kendall."

I quirked an eyebrow "What doesn't feel right?"

"You and him." He mumbled surprising me completely. What the heck?!

I frowned "What's that supposed to mean?"

James stared at me "I just don't feel he's right for you ok? You deserve better." If I was surprised before, then I was absolutely flabbergasted now. And very confused.

I shook my head "Dude you're not making any sense right now."

Suddenly, he stood up and grabbed me by the arms, yanking me towards him. I was scared that he was going to hit me or something and prepared to defend myself when I felt his warm chapped lips on mine.

Fuck.

Fuck.

Fuck.

James was kissing me. Again, what the fuck'?!

I pushed him away so confused. "W-What?"

His eyes were soft "Kendall, I think I like you." And that's how I officially became screwed ladies and gents.

So......................That happened. Vote and comment and forgive my long hiatus guys.

Chapter 25 - Dear One

Sorry guys. I've been dealing with so much stuff right now that it made me want to abandon all my stories and delete this account. But don't panic, I won't.

I'm not much better but in a better situation that before. Maybe I will get better, but I have decided not to abandon this at all because it still gives me the release I need. Thanks so much for all your votes and comments to far and I really do appreciate you all for sitting down and reading whatever unworthy crap I write. Xoxo.

(This chapter is a bit short, but it was necessary.)

Zoe.

My head swirled, processing nothing but a fuzzy haze of confusion. I pushed James away with my pupils dilating and my heart beating at an unnaturally fast rate. He seemed confused by my action with infuriated me on the inside. How dare he even have the guts to appear confused by my action?!

The man I was irrevocably in love with was waiting for me, yet James had the guts to wonder why I refused his advances.

"What the fuck is wrong with you?! Are you stupid?!" I shouted at him.

James blinked breathing hard "I'm sorry K-"

"No you're not!" I shouted back. "You know I have a boyfriend yet you kissed me anyway! FUCK!"

He looked distorted "I'm really sorry, I don't know why I did. I thought it would make me feel something."

I ran hand through my hair roughly going to sit on the carpet near the wall. The fact that my lips had touched someone else's who wasn't Axel made my stomach turn in ten different swirls of disgust.

James was opposite me breathing heavily, his hair covering is eyes. I immediately stood up without thinking and went over to him, hitting him across the face as hard as possibly could. His face showed a mix of shock and pain together.

My hand stung.

"I know that I deserved that. But you have to listen to me Kendall." He pleaded holding up his bruised cheek with his hand.

My breathing was laboured and ragged "Why would you do that?" My voice was thick with emotion.

He stared right at me "You love him that much don't you?"

I didn't answer. I only glared right back at him.

James let out a humorless laugh "I'm so stupid. Fuck, of course you're in love with him. So in love that kissing me disgusts you."

He didn't sound disappointed; more like intrigued about the whole situation.

"Right now I have no explanation owed to you, but yes I love him. I love him so much that it consumes my being and makes me want nothing else. Not you, not any other human on the whole planet."

My phone rang but I ignored it. My head was turning with too many emotions to handle. James sat wearily on the couch, trying not to make eye contact with me. Not that I wanted to anyway.

I walked to the small dining table and snatched my phone.

"Don't expect any form of contact from me ever again. " I said to him without turning back to him. With that statement I left the apartment without a single glance back.

**********"Axel?" I called out as soon as I got into the apartment. My voice was slightly shaky and my fingers trembled slightly as I opened the already unlocked front door. Axel was definitely home by that observation alone. The incident with James made me feel guilty, even though every law in the universe was probably screaming that I wasn't in the wrong.

Still, the fact that someone who wasn't Axel had touched me made me feel as guilty as guilty could be. I closed my eyes and took in a deep breath as I walked into the living room.

I took the bus to get to the apartment seeing as I felt as though my own voice would betray me if I called Axel to send Timothy to pick me up.

The sight of those throw cushions and the maroon sofa brought back memories. I smiled involuntarily as I remembered the first time I came in here. I was as shy as a lamb and could focus on nothing else but how hot Axel was while he stripped in front of me. His sensuous smile was forever etched in my mind and the very thought of the raw passion his eyes held made my legs feel weak.

I sat down on the sofa with my hands folded.

The way his lips glided down my body that night, the emotions that swept through me were too much to handle for me. I groaned silently just thinking about it.

It wasn't just his looks or sex appeal that drew me to him. All that be damned in fact. What I loved was the air around him, that intense respect that he commanded whether he knew it or not. He carried himself like he knew exactly who he was and didn't give a damn what the rest of the world thought.

He didn't try to act unnecessarily tough or strong around me. He never hid any emotion he felt from me with importance that I hadn't known in a long time. He didn't love me like my mom did, trying her best but oblivious to the world around her and the imperfections of her own family. He also didn't love me like my father, living a lie because of the fear of rejection. Maybe Mara loved me once upon a time as her little brother, but that time was long gone. If it ever even existed in the first place.

My fingers brushed the fluffy brown throw pillow. He loved me like Axel. Just the only way he could; true and real and deep down from the heart. Fuck, the people who had said that it was wrong for two men to love each other were severely in the wrong. How could it be wrong to love someone from the very depths of your innermost being? To think about their heart and happiness before your own?

"Kendall?"

That same voice I craved so much called out to me. I turned to hard I could almost hear the whiplash. Axel was standing by the kitchen looking bleary eyed and still in his pajama bottoms.

My heart fluttered knowing that he had been in bed all day, probably still waiting for me.

"Why are sitting here alone?" He asked walking to the living room to join me.

I shrugged "Nothing. Just thinking a little."

"Uh oh." He teased pulling me to wars him. I scoffed a laugh and buried my face in his bare neck.

"So what were you thinking about?" I tensed, thinking carefully before answering.

"About how much I love you."

We both remained silent for almost a minute. Axel's hold on me remained still, not moving an inch.

"I love you Kendall. And I'll love you even more if you take your shoes off the 4000 pound couch." He said sounding serious until the last part.

I laughed removing my Jordans from the sofa. Axel grinned kissing my temple "I love you so much Kendall. If you forget everything else and everyone else in this world, don't forget that."

I nodded, dread forming in the pots of my stomach as I remembered the incident with James. I knew that I should tell him, but at the same time I didn't want our bubble to burst just yet.

"I won't. And I have something to tell you."

He stroked my wrist "Go on."

For the moment, trained my eyes to the floor to ceiling window that showed an immortal like view of London.

"I saw James today."

I felt Axel's eyes move to me. "And?"

"H-He kissed me." The words were bitter and vile in my mouth. My heart rate increased and the tears gathering in my eyes threatened to spill.

I felt him tense, then slowly remove his hold from my body to sit up straight. This was it. He would hate me for good now.

I dared a peek at him to see Axel rubbing his eyes with his hands.

"Kendall. I still love you."

I broke down in tears. He held me once again so my face was directly in his chest muddling my tears.

"I'm so sorry. I'm sorry that I let him. I-I p-p-pushed him away, but he still did. Someone who wasn't you had their lips on mine." I sobbed.

"Kendall I don't blame you. Go's knows it's not your fault in anyway." He said stroking my cheeks.

"I know." I said pitifully.

Axel smiled kissing the corner of my mouth "I'm not mad. Granted I'm not exactly happy by the gesture, but I'm happy that you told me. That you trust me enough."

"Of course I do." I replied matter of factly cleaning my tear streaked face with the sleeve of my jacket. He leaned in and kissed me lightly on the lips, allowing me to deepened it further after a little while. We both pulled away for breath with Axel lying face up on the sofa and me laying down comfortably on his chest. "So you forgive me?" I asked hopefully.

"You didn't do anything wrong. I'm not mad at you at all. I just don't think that I would like to see that James bloke anywhere near you in the present and future."

I smiled into his chest "Yeah. I have something else to tell you?"

"Don't tell me Pierce kissed you too?" He groaned playfully. I laughed slapping his chest lightly "No, that would never happen."

"Then what?"

"Yes I'll move in with you."

Axel broke into the biggest smile I had ever seen and pulled me into a bone crushing hug. I squealed, a very manly squeal, as he kissed every single part of my face.

"Really?"

"Yes!"

He kissed me deeply on the lips. "I have never been this happy in my entire life."

"I'm glad I'm the reason." I stated kissing his move cutely.

"I'll always make it my life's mission to see you happy." Axel said quietly. I placed my head on his chest interlocking our fingers together. "Me too."

Nothing would ever break us apart.

It was short but hope y'all like it. I'm back from the dead ;)

Chapter 26 - Against The World

"You know in a few minutes you're going to have to let go of me." I frowned at Axel's betrayed humor even though my eyes were closed. My arm was currently draped across his chest holding him as close as I could to my body without any intention of doing otherwise. He had woken up a few moments before me and tried to escape to the kitchen but to no avail. Even asleep nothing would allow me to let go of Axel. It wasn't my fault that I had no reason to ever want to let him go. Maybe I was a little clingy, but I damn well didn't care.

He sighed "Babe I need coffee and you'll also need coffee. By waking up and making us some, I'm doing us both a favor." I placed my head on his chest and sighed contently as if all the words which came out of his mouth were equvalient to Minion speak.

Defeated, Axel nuzzled into my neck holding me close to his body. "My little octopus. Guess you finally got your way and kept me here." I smiled into his chest without saying a single word. His hand stroked my naked back contently, dipping lower and lower until he reached the creave of my ass and my breathing hitched slightly.

The previous night had been filled with confessions and assurances. Also some mindblowing love-making also helped the mood a lot. It was baffling how much we both still wanted each other when a lot of couples at this stage were already tired in that aspect of their relationship. But we were far from tired of it. It seemed as though the more we indulged in it, the better it became for the both of us.

I wiggled slightly to make sure that his hand fell right on my ass cheek. He huffed out a laugh "I see what you're doing. Anymore sex and my dick will get stuck in you forever. Besides we're out of lube and condoms."

Now that made me sit up straddling his thighs and glaring down at him "What do you mean no lube? What kind of gay man runs out of lube?"

"Morning to you too love." Axel sarcastically replied. I huffed folding my hands across my chest while laid down lazily with his hands behind his head, smirking like the cat who just got the cream. Of course the very sight made my thighs tremble so I sighed and leaned forward kissing him very sweetly on the lips. "Good Morning my love. Did you sleep well?" "Perfect." He muttered trying to kiss me more. I wasn't sure if he was talking about his sleep or the kiss we were currently sharing. We exchanged more sleepy kisses before I managed to get myself off his body and the bed. "I wish I didn't have to work today." Axel said quietly as I shuffled around his (soon to be our) bedroom. "I just wish we had one more day to ourselves. I'm not ready to share you with the world yet."

His words made me blush as I wore my boxers. "Me neither."

He sat up on the head board "Sadly babe duty calls."

"More like my booty calls." I said seductively swaying my hips as I walked out of the bedroom. If I laughed as he swore at my innuendo, oh well.

***********"Hey mom I tried to use my debit card the other day but it didn't work and the bank said that money was received this month. Please reply when you get this message because I'm sort of worried. Love you."

"Any problem?" Axel asked as soon as I was done with my message to my mom.

I shrugged "Just some money stuff. It's no big deal."

He let his lips linger a bit longer on his coffee cup "Anything I can help with?"

"No I'm fine." I said with a smile interlocking our hands together. He dropped the cup in the sink "But you'll let me know right? If there is a problem."

"Yes I will." I promised holding the lapels of his suit. Axel gave me a chaste kiss on the lips before going to the kitchen island where some of his documents were.

"Am I ever going to meet your parents?"

Now that caught me off guard. I blinked holding my forkful of eggs in mid air. "Huh?"

"You hardly talk about your parents. And you've met my dad. I think it's only fair that I meet your parents." He said casually without looking up from the documents he was sorting through.

He finally looked up "That is if you're serious about us as I think you are."

I dropped my fork and leaned on the kitchen island to properly face him "I am. It's just....... my family is a bit of a tough angle for me. I've actually never taken anyone to meet them."

Axel's expression softened a bit "Sorry I shouldn't have said that way. I just really would like meet your parents, if it's ok with you. We don't have to if you don't want us to."

I held his free hand "We will l. I just need to explain some certain things." My eye wondered to the slim Cartier watch on Axel's wrist. "When you're not about to be late."

He glanced at his watch also "Shit. Guess I gotta go darling." A warm kiss was placed on my lips "I'll see you soon though."

If it was possible. I wouldn't mind holding off talking about my family for a little while longer.

**********It was so ironic how I looked forward to the semester break and now that it arrived, it made me feel useless because I had no idea what to do. Axel was at work so there was no way for him to entertain or keep me busy at the moment. The man did have to earn a living somehow. His millions didn't just fall from the sky.

He still had to work to maintain his lifestyle. To be honest, despite the fact that I would love Axel even if he was dirt poor, it was nice to have a partner who was financially stable. That didn't hurt at all in the practical sense. It wasn't a sole reason, but it was one of the perks.

Currently, I was seated on the couch watching some British soap that wasn't too popular but seemed interesting enough. It also reminded me of Hollyoaks, the soapie that I had caught Pierce sneaking to watch a couple of times with sniffles and Kleenex at his aide. Honestly, he was so much gayer than me.

I watched the show for another additional hour before my phone rang and I picked it up "Hello?"

"Good afternoon. Am I speaking with Kendall Ross?" A deep but familiar voice said.

"Yes you are." I replied muting the tv show that was currently playing.

"This is Detective Palin from the Metropolitan Police Force and I think that we may have some interesting new information about your assault case."

My mouth suddenly felt dry as the memory came back but I did my best to suppress it. "Yes?"

There was some shuffling in the background "I think it would be much more appropriate if you came down to the station for us to discuss." I shut my eyes tightly trying to get a hold of myself "Ok. I'll come in this afternoon."

"Perfect." Detective Palin said before the line went dead. What information could he have now? To be fully honest I wanted to forget the whole incident but a part of me was curious about who would have wanted to hurt me or kidnap me.

I let my thoughts linger a little longer before dialling Axel's number.

"Couldn't wait for me to get home love?" His teasing voice came right on only calming me halfway.

"Somethings come up." I said in an uneasy voice.

"What is it?" He sensed the seriousness in my tone.

I breathed in "There's a new development in the case on my assault and they need to see us at the station soon."

He swore under his breath before calling someone - I assumed was his assistant - to do a few tasks for him.

"Its ok Kendall I'm coming soon. I'll be right with you babe." His words assured me.

I just hoped they would be enough for the dread starting to overwhelm me. Because for some reason I had a feeling that something was about to go wrong and burst our little bubble.

So sorry for the short chapter guys but my life is super hectic once again. I'm literally just squeezing time to write this while studying for my exams in a few months.

Hopefully I have a little more time on my hands soon will try to update sometime next week or this weekend if i can. Thanks for being so patient with me guys.

Zoe.

Chapter 27 - Beautiful Scars On Critical Veins (i)

Song - Underneath - Adam Lambert

The very first time I got on the plane to England, I made a promise to be a good guy and always follow rules. Sure my relatives had always assumed the worst of me and my father, but I was never a troublesome kid.

Never in my life had I ever thought that I would see the inside of police station. Especially not for something like this.

Detective Palin led Axel and I to a small room with a grey door that was his office. Axel held my hand the entire time as if sensing exactly what was going through my mind. He couldn't. Not really anyway. But I'm glad that we were so inline with each other that he knew when things had hit me particularly hard.

The truth was that I didn't know what rattled me so much. Maybe it was the feeling inside that said impending doom was on its way. It might be only exaggerated imagination. Or it could be accurate intuition. Somehow I was hoping that it wouldn't lean unto the later.

Detective Palin adjusted his suspenders before huffing down on his seat. "Take a seat please."

"Thank you." I replied.

Axel had already sat down before permission was granted. My guess was that he didn't particularly feel up to wasting time.

The detective sighed opening his file "The men who assaulted you were questioned repeated and refused to cooperate with us all this while. Which is the main reason your case was delayed for so long. However, after the brilliant suggestion of one of my colleagues, we came up with the impression that they worked for someone above them who they were afraid to reveal. We played them into thinking that the other had confessed about it. Finally we got a suspect."

"And?" Axel inquired holding my hand tighter.

Detective Palin looked straight at me "Kendall, sorry is it alright if I call you by your first name?"

"Very." I replied politely.

He nodded "Have you been in contact with anyone by the name of Gordon Fraiser?"

I frowned in confusion "I've never heard of that name before."

"Exactly as I suspected. But there is someone of particular significance to you who does." He said folding his hands.

"Who detective?" My boyfriend asked, equally as confused.

"Mara Ross."

My blood went cold and my entire body went as stiff as cement "W-What?"

"Babe who is she?" Axel asked in both curiosity and concern at my reaction.

"My sister."

Even I couldn't recognise my own voice. It sounded too hollow, too distant to be mine. "What does she have to do with this?"

He let out a gust of air through his lips "Those men say that your sister ordered that hit on you."

I didn't know then that it was entirely possible for my body to go so cold. I was numb. I couldn't feel anything. Nor could I hear anything. Nothing, but the sound of my belated beating heart.

"I'm sorry you had to find out this way Kendall." Detective Palin said sounding a bit sympathetic at my plight. I didn't even reply him.

"Kendall.... are you ok?" Axel asked hesitantly.

I said nothing nor did I turn to face him.

"Detective are you absolutely sure of what you're saying?" Axel asked again without taking his eyes off me.

"From what I have in these files she's not a pleasant person." He replied thumbing through them. "Mara Ross is wanted for several other things I'm afraid."

That earned a reaction from me. "What?"

He glanced carefully at me "Many of the things she's accused of, I'm not allowed to tell you because it's not in my jurisdiction." I wanted to vomit there and then.

"What business did she have with this Gordon Fraiser guy?" I asked quietly. I would have seemed calm if not for the sight of my cold trembling hands.

Detective Palin seemed hesitant at first.

"Whatever she did almost resulted in my boyfriend almost getting kidnapped so you better damn tell us what it is!!" He said pounding his fist on the table.

The detective remained unfazed at my boyfriend's display "Very well Mr. Gold. Mara Ross is belived to be indebted to Gordon Fraiser and couldn't pay her debts. Since Fraiser is a man known for...... other tastes, she offered him her innocuous and unknowing brother to pay off her debts. According to the testament of his goons. They admitted to following him around and got his address from her."

Now I understand why she had come that day. To prepare me as the sacrifice for her debts. I couldn't even describe what the very memory did to me.

"Dear Lord." Axel murmured in shock. "How could she do that to her own brother?"

"She always hated me." I confessed quietly "But I never thought that us would be this horrible."

In a way I wasn't surprised, but somehow I still was. I knew she hated and blamed me so dearly for everything which happened. But I never thought that the depths of her loathing would get this far as to do this to me. Her baby brother.

"I'm sorry gentlemen but this is what all our evidence points to. Plus Mara Ross is also wanted for certain committed atrocities. I'm fact most parts of this file are under Interpol's jurisdiction so I'm not allowed to even see it." Detective Palin said to us. "B-but why?" I whispered. "Her fiance is very rich so why would she be in debt?"

"Those are questions I can't answer. I've only told you exactly what we've discovered." He replied monotonously. "Even though we don't have enough evidence to get her involved-"

"I want to go home." I announced stunning to two men with me. "I don't want to be here anymore."

"Um are you sure babe?" Axel asked softly trying to hold my hand but I snatched it back surprising the both of us.

"Yes."

The Detective eyed us both awkwardly "Ok then. If I get any other piece of information I'll be sure to contact either of you."

"Thank you Detective." Axel said standing up to shake his hand while I just bolted without waiting or answering any of them. I distantly heard my name being called, probably from Axel, but ignored it without any other thought than the one singularly on my mind.

I got out of the police station onto the chilly street and whipped out my phone from my pocket. Seeing nothing through the hot white fog in my mind, I blindly dialled a number. I waited until it reached voicemail before pouring out my leaking heart out.

"Mara you goddammed bitch! I hope where ever you are, you die a slow painful death because you deserve every bit of it. I've endured every bit of abuse you put me through since I was 14 fucking years old! But this, this is the greatest fucking thing you've pulled through. Congratulations, you've made Satan proud."

People were beginning to give me looks as I shouted into the phone. Not that I blamed them.

My voice trembled "A little bit of me always hoped that you would forgive me for whatever I did, because it wasn't my fault. But now-". My voice lowered significantly as the tears threatened to fall and my eyes blurred up with them. "Now I know that you're a cold hearted witch with no conscience and personally I don't believe we're family at all. Because you're from hell."

The hot tears fell from my eyes and I collapsed on the sidewalk without a care anymore. I was honestly too tired and drained to care anymore.

"Why? Why would she do this to me?" I cried defiantly. I didn't realize how long I'd been sitting there until I felt a pair of warm arms wrap around me.

"I don't know love. But I'll make sure find out. And I'll make sure that she'll never hurt you again." He whispered into my hairline, rocking me back and forth.

I just sat there crying into his chest taking comfort the only way I knew how. From the only person I could take it from.

So I simultaneously wrote this chapter and did my chemistry studying at the same time (awesome multi-tasking I know). Now it's 12:13 am at my side of the world and I have a pounding headache so please let me take my leave and enjoy this chapter.

Comment + vote.

Zoe.

Chapter 28 - Beautiful Scars On Critical Veins (ii)

S ong - Better Than I Know Myself - Adam Lambert.

I don't even need to warn y'all about sexual content anymore. ;) Plus emotional triggers also. Dedicated to because well bae;)

I didn't say a single word as Axel bundled me up into the the backseat of the car.

My face was cold and still wet with tears but I made no movement other than shivering because of how cold it had been on the sidewalk.

Axel had held me without shame as I cried into his chest without lessening his hold on me. That would probably be one of the weakest moments in my life for a long time, but he held me right through it. This man.

"Do you want anything to eat?" He asked softly as we drove home. I shook my head slowly without saying anything. I stared ahead at the dashboard, pretending to focus on the road ahead. In reality, I couldn't focus on anything at all. My mind was blank. Filled with nothing. Void.

We reached the Axel's house a little while later and I sat in the car even after we had stopped until he came to my side and helped me out. After then I blindly followed as he led me up to the penthouse.

"Are you ok?" He asked tentatively as I walked towards the bedroom. I didn't reply to that "I just really want to take a nap."

Axel nodded kissing my forehead gently "You do that. There's something I need to sort out."

I nodded ardently walking to the bedroom and immediately stripping. I didn't even bother wearing my sleep clothes before collapsing unto the bed and into a dreamless sleep.

*********I woke up a few hours and felt a lot better than I did previously. It must have been a pretty long time because I noticed that it was already dark outside.

I blinked sleepily several times before standing up from the bed and exhaling loudly. I looked around the bedroom and saw one of Axel's shirts folded neatly beside my sweatpants on the small table beside his shelf where all the vinyls were arranged. I picked them up wearing them before heading off to the living room where I assumed my boyfriend was currently waiting in.

The nap did make me feel a lot better than I did previously but the incident which occurred earlier weighed heavy in my heart.

I saw Axel, already changed into comfy clothes, in the kitchen dishing up what appeared to be a pasta dish. I was internally grateful that he took up the initiative to make dinner since I was not in the mood at all. I walked carefully not wanting to alert him of my presence then wrapped my arms around his waist and breathed his earthy but still sharp cologne in. "Hi."

Axel, only slightly startled, turned around and hugged me "How do you feel love?"

"A bit better now." I replied snuggling into his chest. We both knew that I wasn't talking about the Mara thing at all in reference to feeling better.

He held me for a little while longer before kissing my forehead "Come on. You need to eat something."

I grumpily agreed dragging my feet to the polished dining table instead of the breakfast bar where we usually ate mostly if we were alone.

He placed the surprising appetizing pasta tomato and cheese petinni in front of me with a glass of water before setting one down for himself. I dug in hungrily since I hadn't eaten for a while.

Axel watched me closely as we both ate in silence. The silence wasn't uncomfortable; it was more of a build-up of what I knew was coming eventually.

I finished eating and stood up with my plates and grabbed Axels since he had also finished eating. He tried to stop me "It's fine I can do it."

"No just let me do it please." I said making a silent plea with my eyes. He allowed me to take it and I cleared up our plates, dropping them in the sink and fetching his expensive scotch from the cupboard with two glasses.

When I turned back, he had relocated to the maroon couch so I moved there and dropped the bottle of scotch and glasses on the coffee table, pouring the both of us each a glass of an acceptable amount. I handed Axel a glass "Thanks." He said sipping it immediately.

I took a sip of the seemingly dry and tingly drink which burned down my throat as I swallowed it. At least I needed the burn.

"So....where do you want me to start from?" I asked sitting on the couch in a manner that I would be sitting exactly opposite from him.

He let out a gust of air "From any part of this story that makes sense."

I nodded looking down in my glass "When my mother and father got married, they were both happy." I started glancing at Axel to make sure that he was paying attention. He was.

"My mother loved my dad utterly and my dad really cherished and care for her. The only thing she failed to realize on time was that my dad wasn't so much in love with her and that he was actually gay."

There was a painful silence that followed due to the shock of my words.

I knew that Axel was itching to ask me questions but held it in himself for the sake of allowing me finish my tale. I took a large gulp of the scotch, because I needed it intensely and poured myself another glass. All through my boyfriend remained perfectly still.

"Don't get me wrong: my dad did love and care for her intensely. His reasons for marrying a woman despite his orientation was due to his overbearing Catholic family and his need to please them. My mother found out quite early in their relationship and although she was hurt, she agreed to remain married to him because even if they weren't romantically involved, they had become to best of friends." I paused taking another sip.

"All through their marriage my parents never cheated on each other, never had any major fights and remained in perfect harmony even when they had Mara and I." I said looking directly at Axel knowing that may story was about to reach its climax.

"My sister was the epitome of a perfect daughter. Awesome grades, perfectly balanced social life, head of all the best clubs and a string of rich and connected boyfriends. She wasn't very hateful towards me then, but she wasn't ever find of me really. Mostly because I couldn't keep up with her, or bask her in the attention she needed. Mara was so used to the attention showered on her by admirers and onlookers. She was like a peacock; the attention made her even greater."

I sighed taking a deep gulp and another deep breath. Axel stood up and moved towards my side of the couch so he would be directly next to me. Which I was grateful for.

"Then around 14, I had my first boyfriend and she found out."

"Mara?" He questioned. I nodded "And she was livid. In her mind something of that scale would cause problems and a great scandal in my family. Apart from my father's strictly religious side, most people from my mothers side weren't very liberal minded and most likely wouldn't accept it. And she of course didn't need a discrepancy like that tainting our perfect family."

"So she threatened me. Told me to break up with my boyfriend or she would make things hard for me. I didn't of course and that made her mad. That was when her distreatment and hatred of me began. Sneering and picking on me every single time she could. She even tried to get her college friends to sleep with me and 'change' me but it never worked out."

I closed my eyes trying not to reminisce on those times. "Then we broke up and she was happy. But I wasn't anyway. She told me that if I ever thought of being anything but straight, she would end my life." Axel placed his arm around my shoulder calming me gently.

"One day I was tired of the hold she had over me and during a large Christmas dinner in my uncle's house with our extended family, I came out and said that I was gay." I played with the time of my fingers. It was strange that telling the story, I still felt the emotions that went through me then, now. The fear, pain and utter relief which flooded me at the same time.

"I got so much hate at that moment. Family members who I grew up with scowled in my direction and made comments about how disgusting I was. My parents were shocked and my sister was fuming. She tried to put it off and told everyone I was joking and that I was just playing a huge prank on all of them. Then I insisted that I wasn't."

"She screamed at me and I ran away from the house into the road in fear all alone. It was after 15 minutes of wandering that my parents found me and held me as I cried in their arms. My father then told me about how he was also gay and revealed it right after I had left. My mother expressed how proud she was of the two of us and how she loved us despite whatever it was on our way home that we got into an accident. And my dad didn't make it."

I didn't realize that I was crying until Axel wiped my face with his thumb and I realized how blurry my sight was. The memories I had locked so long ago being brought back to mind were too much to handle.

"No one visited in the hospital save a few family members and Mara. In the presence of my mother she cried and said she accepted me but in private she promised to make my life a living hell for all I had done to ruin our family. And I couldn't say a thing."

After finishing my story I placed my head in Axels shoulder and cried my heart out for the second time that day. And he comforted me for the second time.

"I love you and nothing would ever make me stop." He assured me kissing every inch of my face he could find.

I sobbed "Sometimes I think it was my fault. That my family hates us and that my dad died -"

"Shhh don't you dare blame yourself for any of this." He said firmly holding my face to his. "Fate is a strange thing and I promise you that none of what happened is your fault. You need to understand that now. Even if you didn't come out something might have happened and tragedy would be struck anyway. But don't you blame yourself when you are clearly the victim of this all."

I cried into his chest without stopping again. "She's hated me so terribly since then. Nothing I ever did changed that."

"Why didn't you ever tell your mother about what Mara did to you all those years?" He asked cleaning my face gently.

It was a question many would ask but I had my reasons.

I sighed pressing my face closer to his chest "Because I couldn't ruin everything for her. Our family became weary of her, her son was a disgraced homosexual and the man she loved died so terribly and couldn't even fully give himself to her. Mara was the only seemingly perfect and normal thing to her. So I decided that it would be wrong of me to fully destroy it all for her."

A warm kiss was placed on my forehead "God you're such a selfless martyr it hurts me to know that you've gone this long, living like this."

I smiled softly despite my tears sitting up to look at him "I've been living like this so I'm used to it."

Axel kissed me gently "Good thing you've met me because I intend to make sure that you know what it's like to be taken care of. Physically and emotionally."

I held his cheek "Thank you." Fuck as if it wasn't already enough that I loved Axel already, he gives me more reasons to adore him. My life story and reason for not trusting anyone was locked so tightly within me and I refused to share it with anyone else until he came along.

"I love you." I whispered as he leaned in for another kiss. He gladly took it in, holding my waist and pressing all his love down into me. I wrapped my arms around his neck, kissing him as hard as I could.

He gently laid me down on the couch, pushing my shirt up to reveal my soft skin and placed a kiss right there.

"It's now my job to protect you and I'll do it as long as I can." He confessed caressing my stomach with his lips.

My eyes fluttered and I let out a gentle moan pushing up his face to look at me "And I'll always protect you also. Because I'll always protect those I love."

He groaned sending another deep kiss my way. I ran my fingers through his silky smooth hair trying to taste even more of him. He pulled my sweatpants down and rubbed around my pale thighs.

"Fuck." I whispered enjoying his touch shamelessly. Axel knelt up removing his own shirt and pants and tossed them all on the furry carpet in the living room.

"I want you so much. I want to taken care of you so much." He said kissing every visible inch of my skin that he could find. I arched my body to his kisses and cherished the feel of him. He brought out a container of lube from the side of the couch confusing me "When did that get there?" I asked.

"As you complaining?" He asked raising an eyebrow.

I shook my head quickly "Not at all." By now we were both hard and our erections rubbed against each other, causing a series of groans and moans.

He placed his lube slicked fingers into my hole, fingering me to prepare me for himself. I moaned so wantonly, bucking my hips to his touch and holding his shoulders harder. Axel teased my nipple, sucking it hard as he fingered me at the same time.

"Need you in me now." I breathed out. "Well your wish is my command." Axel replied with a sexy smile, stroking his cock with the lube before positioning himself in me. We hadn't used a condom since the incident with Laura. I had tested myself every six months even though I hadn't had sex since I was seventeen and Axel had produced a test result for me a month into our relationship.

He kissed me gently first "I would do anything for you." Before thrusting in so powerfully I screamed. I tightened my legs around his waist and gasped as he thrusted again and again.

"Oh fuck." I moaned closing my eyes tight as he kissed my neck, thrusting and grunting in unison.

"Oh babe, how the hell are you so tight?" Axel groaned into my mouth littering kisses all around.

"Only you." I replied making him thrust faster than before.

We were a sexy tangle of sweat and limbs on the couch, enveloping ourselves together the best way we knew how. When I was halfway to my orgasm, Axel carried me up and laid on his back placing me on top so that I could ride him. I groaned at the intensity of our new position and began to ride him out like a mad person.

"Kendall! Babe!" He shouted digging his fingers into my thighs trying to match his the thrusts with mine.

I panted looking down at him and leaning downward to kiss him "I love you so much Axel."

"Same my love." He replied thrusting particularly hard into me. Two strokes of my cock and I was coming all over his chest with a whimper.

"My beautiful boy." Axel sighed before cumming right inside me. I collapsed on top of him, panting hard at the rigorous love making we had just done.

"There you go again. Frying my brain and such." I murmured making him chuckle. He wrapped one arm around me and used to other to bring down the Afghan from the top of the couch and cover us both.

"I'll always be here Kendall." Axel promised as I snuggled into his chest. And somehow, that was the first time in a while I had fully and while trusted someone's words.

Ayo people! Hope you loved reading this as much as I loved writing this. I love this boys so much in wish they were real so that I could keep them but alas :(

Don't be afraid to send feedback on this chapter and vote as much as you can. Also, check out my new story Serendipity on my profile. Good day.

Zoe

Chapter 29 - Take A Breath, Say You Love Me

Song - Tough Love - Jessie Ware.

I was startled awake in the middle of the night by a slight movement next to me. I forced my eyes open trying to make out the movement in darkness.

My heart slightly jumped at the sight of the dark silhouette but I quickly eased up when I realized that it was just Axel sitting down by the edge of the bed.

"You're the most beautifully person I've seen naked you know." I said softly wanting him to know that I was now awake but not startle him. His back muscles flexed slightly. "Sorry to wake you up."

"It's ok." I replied sitting up to drape myself on his back. "Now tell me what's got you up."

I could feel Axel tense up once again but I held on to him anyway. He sighed "My mom was the only who could ever make me eat vegetables without puking for the first eight years of my life."

I immediately sat beside him so that I could survey his face properly "There was always something... warm about her. Warm and safe. Like even if the whole world made me believe something was wrong and she told me that it was right, I would believe only her."

I knew that it was hard. Really hard for Axel to tell me something that had eaten him alive for so long. It wasn't a story he happily shared to all ears, even without that much of a hint I could tell. Maybe it was my own confession or something he thought of that spurred this confession out of him. But whatever it was made me grateful, because it meant that he would finally be free with me. That this haunting part of him was free towards me.

I laid my head on his arm as he continued "Maybe that's what made everything else so much harder. When she died. Because I had grown up thinking of her as invincible, a superhero of sorts."

He let out a humorless laugh "Lots of people call their dads their hero but for me, my mother was my heroine. My defender against all things. The monsters under my bed and the ones I faced outside my room."

I caressed his arm without interrupting "But I guess that every superhero had their kryptonite. And hers was in form of a needle or pill."

Ah. There it was.

"My mother was a drug addict." He was quiet after that. It took me a good ten seconds to feel the warm tears on my face from leaning on him. I sat up and hugged him as tight as I could feeling my own tears resurfacing again.

"She was depressed. She was withdrawn from my dad, from me. I still can't get the details of why she was that way. It's something that my dad and I can't even talk about today." Axel said holding on to my body to stop himself from crying even more.

"It hurts now because I couldn't see it. Not until it was too late when she overdosed. I'll never forget that day Kendall. For the first time she was cold, so very cold. All her warmth had left for good when I found her."

He finally let go and sobbed right into my arms. I didn't see him as weak or not manly for his tears. All I saw him was as real, as raw and just as Axel. That was what convinced me that I was the only person who had truly loved him. While Lauren and the rest of the world saw the untouchable, smirking man in a suit, I saw the man who cried like a child without shame in my arms. The man who loved my mother unconditionally. The man who loved me unconditionally.

"Thank you." I whispered. "Thank you for telling me."

He looked up at me with his red-rimmed eyes "No thank you. You stayed."

I rubbed his nape "You told me to stay, that day on the yacht. That you would tell me if I stayed. So I did."

Axel kissed me softly "Yeah you did."

"That's why your dads charity is called Warm Hands right?" I asked cautiously. He nodded looking down briefly at his own hands "It was really his idea for the name. To help people.... also hurting like that. So that no one ever loses the person with warm hands in their life to drugs."

"You're amazing." I told him with a smile on my face.

He snorted shaking his head "I love you. Thank you for staying."

"And I'm never leaving." I whispered against his lips. "No matter what, I'm never leaving."

"Me neither." He whispered back before pressing his lips against mine again. And that was how we stayed up kissing like idiots in love up until dawn.

****

"I never really noticed the awesome view you had up from here." I commented looking down at the city from Axels amazing floor to ceiling windows in his office.

He snorted from his desk still looking over his files "Gets boring after a while trust me."

"Nah I don't think so." I said cheekily. "It's like being Batman. Surveying the city from your tower of power." I walked over to his desk sitting down on his lap carelessly. Axel had to come to the office because there were a few things he needed to sort out urgently. Even offering sex on a silver platter couldn't keep him at home. But thankfully they weren't too hectic so I could accompany him.

His arms automatically wrapped themselves around my waist "Well you must be Batgirl then became that arse of yours is just too good not to be."

"Right." I answered dryly at his sexist comment. "Remember that comment when I make you sleep on the couch tonight. With getting any. At all."

He chuckled leaning back on his chair "See? You're even threatening to withhold sex. Clearly the Batgirl of this duo."

"Eh eh. You're on thin ice already." I warned making him raise his hands in mock defeat. We remained comfortably silent as I sat on his lap while he worked.

"You ok?" I asked remembering the early morning confessions. Axel sighed without looking up from the document he was signing "Aren't I supposed to also be asking you that?"

I shook my head "I'm fine. Besides I'm more worried about you right now." I placed my hand on his cheek to caress it gently.

After last night and this morning it seemed as though we had emerged something new from our relationship. We both unlocked each other's most guarded weaknesses and remained through it. That had further strengthed our love as far as I had noticed.

He tilted his head to press an long kiss into my palm that made my body tingle "Kendall..... you have to tell your mother about Mara."

I stood up from his lap abruptly "Not a chance."

Axel blew a gust of air "Babe-"

"No ok. I'm not doing that to her. I can't do that to her." I said firmly. I knew that sometime I might have to reveal all that Mara had done to me. But with the whole case and the fact that I still had to relay my side of the story to Detective Palin, my head wanted a break away from all thoughts of my sister for a little while longer.

He stood up from his chair and walked to where I stood placing his hands on both of my shoulders "You've done so many selfless things in your life Kendall. I admire that. But your sister is a wanted criminal now and sooner than later she will get caught. And your mother will definitely find out by then. Isn't it better she hears it from you now?"

I hesitated "I... I can't just spring it up on her after all this time. What if she hates me for doing all of this?"

He lifted up my chin "Love, you've held this within yourself since you were 15. I'd say that no one has the right to hate you for staying out that long because of how much you love your mother. But you can't keep suffering any longer. You have to tell her my love."

I sighed closing my eyes "Fine..... I'll think about it."

He kissed me chastely but sweetly enough "Good."

"Now when are we going to start moving my stuff?" I asked eager to change the subject.

Axel shrugged "Honestly I was waiting for your decision. I already have a moving truck on stand by."

I rolled my eyes fondly. Axel was nothing if not an over eager puppy.

"Well sometime before the winter break ends. It'll be stressful if we do it after the new semester begins." I suggested sitting on the couch in his office.

He shrugged "Whenever. You make the call and I'll gladly do your bidding."

I let out a chuckle then "Can't believe I was ever afraid of you. You're too cute to be real."

Axel of course rolled his eyes then narrowed them "Don't go spreading that information around."

I smiled innocently.

His phone rang. He picked up with the usual "Axel Gold speaking." That made me swoon internally. But his face darkened slightly at whatever was said on the phone making my heart jump.

"Ok we'll be there." He replied quickly, trying to calm the person on the other end of the line before dropping his phone.

"What's wrong?" I asked with all the possibilities making my stomach fall from within.

"It was Martin. Spencer is in the hospital. Something is wrong with him."

Dun dun dun.......... what's happening with Spencer? Do you think Kendall should tell his mom about Mara? Tell us in your comments.

There's also an update for The Wanted Ones for those of you who are interested in that one and another update for Rock Me is also coming pretty soon. Also my new book Serendipity is coming with its first chapter in a little while. Hope you guys enjoy :)

Zoe.

Chapter 30 - Exhale

S ong - Hold My Hand - The Fray

I consider this my late birthday present to you all. Enjoy ;).

I had never seen Axel so ruffled all the while I'd known him. I knew that he and Spencer were best friends for a long time and that he would do anything for him. But once we received the frantic call from a sobbing Martin, he rushed out with me on his heels, barely barking out any coherent orders to Stacey and called Timothy who was luckily on stand by at the time.

"Axel please breathe. You're shaking." I said once I noticed his shaky hands trying to grip unto his cell phone.

"W-what could have happened?" He asked in a panicked voice. "He was eating right and exercising properly according to Martin-"

"We'll find out soon. He'll be fine. I'm sure he'll be fine." I said to reassure him even though I wasn't so sure myself. Axel buried his face in my neck taking a few deep breaths before I realized that we hadn't moved and Timothy probably was still wondering where we were going since neither of us uad told him anythung. I had to give him props for acting completely unaffected even as his boss was having a breakdown behind him.

"Did Martin tell you where the hospital was?" I asked softly.

"St. Mary's. " He murmured. Timothy obviously heard because he began driving then without waiting for any of us to say anything else.

During the drive to the hospital, I hoped inwardly within myself that Spencer would be fine. I really didn't know him as well as did Martin but I wanted him to recover as much as everyone else.

We reached the hospital in record time and Axel rushed us to the main reception where he asked for where Spencer was staying. She directed us to the third floor where there were a bunch of private wards.

I immediately saw Martin and Shorty in the waiting area. Martin leaned against the wall with his eyes red and sniffing while Shorty sat down dabbing a Kleenex to her face occasionally.

"Oh thank goodness you're here!" Martin said launching himself into Axels open arms as soon as we were spotted. Axel held him close as the boy sobbed into his shirt.

I slipped next to Shorty and placed my hand in hers since she seemed to be the only coherent one at the moment "What happened? Did they say?"

She shook her head "All we heard was that some delivery van hit him but we haven't heard anything since he was brought in half an hour ago. I was with Martin when we got the news."

A short plump lady in scrubs who I assumed was the doctor came in shortly after "Family of Spencer Hale?"

Martin jumped forward from Axels arms like a pumped up balloon without waiting for anyone else to speak "We're here. What's wrong with him?"

The woman eyed him warily "Are you his immediate family?"

"I'm his boyfriend. He doesn't have any immediate family." Martin said and I was scared that the poor boy was going to burst into tears once again if this lady didn't let us pass through.

She nodded looking down at her clipboard "Well he's stable. No real damage except his broken arm and a few bruises so I'd say he must be really lucky. Especially since that truck hit him so close to impact."

It seemed as though we all let out the huge breath we were holding in. Both Axel and Shorty looked relieved. Martin smiled for the first time since we arrived.

"Can we see him?" Martin asked. The doctor smiled and nodded "Of course he's in ward 312. Come this way please."

She led us through the wards until we reached 312. Spencer was lying down wearing a hospital gown with his broken arm slung across his chest with a nurse attending to him. He looked a little better than I had expected. His face softened up at the sight of Martin "Baby."

Martin sobbed again and ran right towards his bed hugging him but carefully so at not to cause him anymore pain. "I was so scared. When they called me I was scared."

"Baby it's ok." Spencer cooed at him brushing his forehead with his good hand "I'm fine. See? Just got a bit unlucky?"

Axel snorted "I'll say." Ah, so worried, scary Axel was gone so soon? Spencer playfully rolled his eyes at him but I knew that he was happy at his presence. Shotty folded her arms "If you weren't already in pain, I'd punch you myself for being so careless."

"Not if I do it first." Martin said suddenly glaring at his boyfriend. "Why the hell would you cross the road without looking first? Are you trying to give me my first heart attack before I'm even thirty?"

Spencer looked a bit sheepish "Well to be honest I was a bit excited so looking out on the road wasn't my first priority."

"And what got you excited enough to want to die?" Shorty asked with a snort.

Spencer reached for something in the drawer next to his bed "I was I'd get to do this when I'm not high on morphine, but what the hell right?"

It was a small velvet box. I think all our hearts dropped at the same time.

"Martin, ever since the day I first me you at that stupid firm party when I made partner, I've always been intrigued by you. Your unique sense of style, your fascinating way of living, your sweet and wonderful heart. I was hoping that even though you're younger and hotter than me, you wouldn't mind spending the rest of your life with this boring old man?"

He smiled hopefully at Martin and opened the box with his thumb "Martin Henry Doyle, will you marry me?"

Martin squealed and hugged with all his strength causing Spencer to wince a little. We all clapped and smiled, even nurse who was there the while time.

"I can't believe this." Martin said as Spencer carefully slid the ring on his finger with his good hand and kissed his fiance's ring finger "I can believe it. I've been planning this for about two weeks now." Martin kissed him hard at that admission.

"Hey no rough games yet." Shorty warned but she was smiling also.

"Congrats guys." Axel said interlocking his fingers with mine. I smiled warmly at them "Least you didn't get hit for nothing."

"Hey that doesn't mean you should get hit by cars every time you want to do something big like this." Martin warned.

My phone vibrated in my pocket. I picked it up to check the ID and it was my mom. I kissed Axel on the cheek and excused myself "I'll be back."

I went out of the room to the middle of the hallways where there was no one. I wasn't sure whether to answer or not because I didn't know of she had heard about the incident with Mara.

I answered the call "Hello mom?"

"Hello sweetheart." Her voice didn't show any indication that she was worried or heard any disturbing news. "Is everything alright mom?"

"Yes. I just want know if you're still coming down for Christmas?" I was evidently relieved. She didn't know anything yet. "Yeah I will."

"Good. I hope I'll also be able to get Mara. She's too busy nowadays." Yes, making deals with criminals.

"Ok mom. I will. Love you." I said.

"Love you too my boy." She said softly. The line went dead. I knew that I had to tell her now. It had gone for too long. I would be the greatest villain ever, if i willing deceived my mother like this, even though the outcome would hurt her in the end.

"You ok?" I was a bit startled until I knew who it was then I relaxed. Axel placed his hand on my shoulder "You just left. Wanted to be sure you're ok."

I hugged him tightly "I'm ok. I'm ok."

www.ingramcontent.com/pod-product-compliance
Lightning Source LLC
Chambersburg PA
CBHW072149070526
44585CB00015B/1055